They Saw the Invisible

The Heroes of Hebrews 11

Claudia Barba

They Saw the Invisible
The Heroes of Hebrews 11

All quotations from the Bible are from the New King James Version.

Print: ISBN 978-0-9914576-6-3

Ebook: eISBN 978-0-9914576-7-0

Cover and layout design by Jennifer Lassiter

Cover photo by Dave Barba

Dedication

To our children

Stephanie, Susannah, and Jeremiah

I have no greater joy than to hear that
my children walk in truth.
(3 John 1:4)

Table of Contents

Before We Begin

Though we call Hebrews a book, it is actually a letter. It is one of the twenty-one epistles in the New Testament—and the most intriguing.

We do not know who wrote the letter to the Hebrews. Guesses have ranged from Paul to Apollos to Barnabas, from Luke to Silas to Philip to the married couple Priscilla and Aquila. Of these, Paul seems the most likely, but since we cannot be sure, for convenience we will just call the writer *he*. Whoever he was, he was skillful with the Greek language, familiar with Hebrew history and culture, and passionate about Jesus. His heart connection with his readers and his use of the Old Testament to reason with them suggest that, like them, he was a Jew.

We also do not know who received this letter or where they lived. There is a hint that the writer wrote from Italy (Heb. 13:24), but his readers could have been anywhere from Judea to Spain. Some of them may have been on the fringes of faith—seekers rather than disciples, born into Jewish families but not yet born into the family of God—but it's likely that most of them were believers in Jesus as the Messiah.

We are not sure when Hebrews was written, but we can guess. Since sacrifices were still being brought to the temple (Heb. 10:1, 11), we know it was written before the AD 70 destruction of Jerusalem, probably just a few years earlier than that.

Jesus lived on earth until about AD 33, so when Hebrews was penned, the miracles, crucifixion, and resurrection of Jesus were still fresh news. The people reading this epistle could have seen Jesus in person or known people who did (Heb. 2:3). They could have met the traveling apostles, heard them preach, and witnessed their miracles. With so much firsthand testimony available, you would think these early believers would find it easy to be steadfast in their faith. But some of them were struggling. It is easy to see why.

For several decades, they had been expecting Jesus to return, as He had promised: "I will come again and receive you to Myself; that where I am, there you may be also" (John 14:3). They watched and waited, believing that any day, any minute, Jesus would arrive to take them away to be with Him. But He didn't.

The delay must have seemed long (it still does). As they waited, life grew harder. Jewish believers were being disowned by their families and called crazy by their friends. Some were assaulted and arrested, so harshly treated that they ran away to live in strange but safer places. Growing persecution made their martyrdom increasingly likely. Being believers in this Messiah, they could see, was not going to be easy.

Meanwhile, community life continued as usual. Jewish family events revolved around the calendar of religious feasts and sacrifices, but since these Jesus-followers now worshiped only "in spirit and in truth" (John 4:21-24), they were excluded from occasions they used to enjoy. They had already given up so much to follow Christ. Now, facing a future that promised even more sorrow and pain, some began drifting back to their old ways of worship.

Then this letter arrived. Gathered in small groups, believers listened as over and over the writer urged, "Don't give up. Don't go back. Even with all your losses and loneliness, sorrow and suffering, life in Christ is still far better than your old life under the Law."

The writer assured them that God had not abandoned them. Instead, through their suffering He was giving them the privilege of joining a band of heroes—a congregation of people who had held steadfastly to their faith through whatever came and were now receiving their reward. Those heroes are the men and women of Hebrews 11.

Hebrews is more than just an anonymous letter written to an unknown group of people over two thousand years ago. It is a message from God to you! Though the words that poured out of the writer's mind and heart onto the page were shaped by his individual experiences and abilities and applied to specific circumstances, the writer was so guided and inspired by the Holy Spirit that every sentence speaks eternal truth. God is the ultimate author of Hebrews, and like all of scripture, it is for your good.

> All scripture is given by inspiration of God, and is profitable for doctrine, for reproof, for correction, for instruction in righteousness, that the man of God may be complete, thoroughly equipped for every good work. (2 Tim. 3:16-17)

One portion of Hebrews, chapter eleven, was written to help us understand faith. Faith matters, for it links our hearts to invisible truth. By faith we see the God Who made us and died for us. By faith we trust His grace for forgiveness of sin. By faith we stake our eternity on His promises. Faith makes the Christian life possible.

Hebrews 11 will be home base as we travel through the Bible visiting with the heroes of faith who parade across its verses. We will watch these men and women make decisions and handle crises. We will listen in on their conversations with God. As we review the life stories of these fallible but faithful people, we will learn to do what they did: see the invisible and live by what we see.

A teacher's guide/answer key is available as a free download here: https://ipresson.com/hebrews-11-book-study-guide/

CHAPTER ONE
The Heart of Faith

Now faith is the substance of things hoped for, the evidence of things not seen. For by it the elders obtained a good testimony. (Heb. 11:1-2)

Faith is a simple but complex, familiar but extraordinary word. There are illustrations and principles of faith on every page of the Bible, but Hebrews 11 holds the heart of what God wants us to know about faith. The word *faith* appears only a few times in the Old Testament but hundreds of times in the New Testament. How many times can you find this word in Hebrews 11?

There's no doubt about the theme of this chapter! It begins with a much-loved verse, which is the only straightforward definition of faith in the Bible. Here God tells us what faith *is*.

Now faith is

If you were asked to give a synonym for *faith,* you might choose a word like *assurance, trust, belief, reliance,* or *confidence.* Though those words are close in meaning, there is no perfect synonym for this profound word.

The New Testament word translated *faith* is the Greek word *pistis.* In the Bible, it especially means the faith that saves. Have you been saved? Have you believed that Jesus died on the cross for you and received His gift of eternal life? That took faith—saving faith.

> For by grace you have been saved through faith, and that not of yourselves; it is the gift of God. (Eph. 2:8)

Look at 2 Corinthians 13:5 and 2 Timothy 4:7. In these scriptures, *pistis* is used in a different way. What is "the faith"? Why do you think it is called that?

the substance

In Greek this word is *hupostasis.* That's a concrete reality like a strongly-built building, a carefully-worded contract, or a solid-rock promise—things tested and found worthy of trust. Faith gives reality, or substance, to the intangibles we believe.

In Hebrews 3:14, *hupostasis* is translated *confidence.* Think of the way you can march along a concrete sidewalk as compared to stumbling across a swaying rope bridge and you'll get the picture. Faith helps us live confidently by giving us assurance that what we believe will not fail.

In Hebrews 1:3, Jesus is called the *hupostatis*—the substance—of God. People who saw Jesus were seeing the physical manifestation of the God Who is spirit (John 4:24). Jesus was our invisible God made visible, our unseeable God appearing in human form.

> That which was from the beginning, which we have heard, which we have seen with our eyes, which we have looked upon, and our hands have handled, concerning the Word of life—the life was manifested, and we have seen, and bear witness, and declare to you that eternal life which was with the Father and was manifested to us. (1 John 1:1-2)

After seeing and touching Jesus' resurrected body, the disciple Thomas cried out, "My Lord and my God!" Thomas believed because he saw, and Jesus praised him (John 20:26-29). Who else does Jesus praise? (See John 20:29.)

That's you—and every believer who, even without up-close experiences like the apostles had, has faith in invisible truths like the incarnation. Blessed are you, when your beliefs are grounded in faith rather than sight!

of things hoped for

The hope faith gives is more than a longing for something to happen someday. Faith's hope is a firm expectation for the future, based on what has happened before and what is happening right now. Faith makes the future as real as the past and present.

> Therefore, having been justified by faith, we have peace with God through our Lord Jesus Christ, through whom also we have access by faith into this grace in which we stand, and rejoice in hope of the glory of God. (Rom. 5:1-2)

Which blessing was accomplished by God for you—by faith—the moment you were saved?

Which blessings are yours right now—by faith?

Which one are you still waiting for—by faith?

Your past and present blessings are invisible but real, and so is your future in heaven.

Imagine you bought a new house yesterday. (Congratulations!) You know it is yours based on what happened yesterday: you signed a stack of papers and gave somebody piles of money. Though you are not yet living in it, the house is yours, and the joy of ownership is as real as if you had already moved in. You want to celebrate!

While I was getting acquainted with a new friend, I asked her where she was from. "I'm from Michigan," she answered, then paused and added, "but that's not my real home." Right away I knew what she meant. We were sisters in Christ, children of the same Father, looking forward to our real home in heaven.

Heaven is as real as any city in Michigan. Our heavenly home is not bought with money, and we do not have to build it ourselves. It's the free gift of His grace through our faith. That is something to celebrate!

the evidence

Evidence is proof that leads to a conclusion—so how can faith be called evidence? Aren't faith and proof opposites?

Skeptics think so. They disparage Christianity by calling it an unprovable, irrational religious system based on superstition and fantasy rather than logic and reason. *The Genesis story of creation? Unscientific! God becoming a man? Impossible! Jesus rising from the grave? Absurd! Forget this faith stuff. Give us proof!*

The realities of Christianity are not provable in the way unbelievers demand, for its truths are far greater than eyes can see or minds can conceive. Our faith is not unreasonable; it is beyond reason. It is not subject to the natural mind; it is supernatural.

Who are three reliable witnesses to the truth? (See 1 John 5:6-7.)

How has truth been made available to us? (See 2 Pet. 1:20-21.)

How do we know what God says is true? (See Titus 1:2, Num. 23:19.)

If we doubt His words, what are we doing? (See 1 John 5:10.)

> Faith is believing the unreasonable, the impossible, and the unexplainable, because someone else in whom we have absolute

confidence has said it was so, and upon his word we believe it, without asking any further proof.[1]

Like written testimony accepted as evidence in a courtroom, the written Word of God is a reliable witness to truth. If you know what the Bible says, you know truth, for the scriptures are absolute and undeniable. They are more reliable than senses, feelings, or intellect. Independent of time and circumstances, they never change and can never be destroyed.

> Forever, O Lord, Your word is settled in heaven. (Psa. 119:89)

> The entirety of Your word is truth, and every one of Your righteous judgments endures forever. (Psa. 119:160)

> The grass withers, the flower fades, but the word of our God stands forever. (Isa. 40:8)

There is one more powerful witness to truth—a changed life. Altered attitudes and desires are witnesses to the miraculous inward transformation called the new birth. No one can see salvation, but everyone can see the changes salvation brings.

> Therefore, if anyone is in Christ, he is a new creation; old things have passed away; behold, all things have become new. (2 Cor. 5:17)

Though your intellect and will were involved when you decided to follow Christ, your salvation did not come through logic or reason, so it cannot be destroyed by them. I know a young woman whose Christian beliefs are continually mocked and challenged by people close to her. Unshaken, she says, "Asking me to deny or abandon my faith is like asking me to be un-born. I am, and always will be, God's own beloved child." Her calm confidence is a powerful proof of the invincible, life-changing power of faith.

of things not seen

Our God is invisible (1 Tim. 1:17), except through faith in Jesus Christ.

---

[1] M.R. De Haan, *Hebrews* (Grand Rapids: Zondervan Publishing House, 1959), 150.

> No one has seen God at any time. The only begotten Son, who is in the bosom of the Father, He has declared Him. (John 1:18)

> He who sees Me sees Him who sent Me. (John 12:45)

Our God is eternal. No one made Him. But He made everything else, and all His creation, whether visible or invisible, is as real as He is. His Word tells us so.

> For by Him all things were created that are in heaven and that are on earth, visible and invisible, whether thrones or dominions or principalities or powers. All things were created through Him and for Him. (Col. 1:16)

> While we do not look at the things which are seen, but at the things which are not seen. For the things which are seen are temporary, but the things which are not seen are eternal. (2 Cor. 4:18)

How long will visible things last?

How long will invisible things last?

Which of these does faith focus on?

For by it the elders

What is *it*?

These elders are not church leaders, but patriarchs and prophets, the forefathers of the Hebrews reading this letter. These men offered sacrifices as symbols of their faith that a Messiah would come, but they were not redeemed by the blood of their animals. They were saved by believing in the perfect Lamb that one day would come as the final offering for sin.

> For it is not possible that the blood of bulls and goats could take away sins. (Heb. 10:4)

The Jewish elders looked forward to the coming of the Messiah. We look back to Bethlehem and Calvary, but otherwise our faith is the same as theirs. Like them, "we have been sanctified through the offering of the body of Jesus Christ once for all" (Heb. 10:10), through "the precious blood of Christ, as

6

of a lamb without blemish and without spot" (1 Pet. 1:19).

obtained a good testimony.

The testimony the elders received was a *martureo*, or report card. The world gave them failing grades, but God gave their faith an excellent report, and His evaluation is always accurate.

Think it through

Answer in your own words: what is faith?

With that as God's standard, what grade would He give your faith?

CHAPTER TWO
The Starting Line of Faith: Creation

By faith we understand that the worlds were framed by the word of God, so that the things which are seen were not made of things which are visible. (Heb. 11:3)

In chapter one, we learned what faith *is*. Now we'll begin discovering what faith *does*. The first thing it does is obvious but true: *faith believes!* In this chapter we will walk slowly through the words of just one verse, Hebrews 11:3, to find out why believing in God's creation of all things matters so much.

By faith we understand that the worlds were framed

The worlds are all that exists, has ever existed, or ever will exist in time and space, everything seen or unseen, material or spiritual—everything and everyone except God, Who had no beginning and will have no end.

To *frame* is to arrange, or assemble, from already-existing materials. When you "make" dinner, you don't begin by creating food. You gather ingredients you have grown and harvested or bought and brought home. Then you *frame* (chop, stir, blend, bake) them into something delicious. When I "make" a quilt, I don't start by creating cloth. I buy ready-made fabrics, cut them into pieces, then sew them back together in a new way, *framing* them until my quilt looks (more or less) like my pattern.

Arranging and altering what has already been made is the best we human "creators" can do. Though we can split and combine atoms, we cannot construct them. We can change the shape of matter from solid to liquid to gas to plasma and back again, but we cannot create, or even destroy, matter. Even the most brilliant humans have limits.

But the Creator has no limits. First, He created all the elements of the universe *ex nihilo*—from nothing. From those original components, He framed, or arranged, everything in the world to look and function the way He planned. Believing this is the starting point of faith.

by the word of God

Which member of the Trinity was the special agent of creation? (See Heb. 1:1-2, Col. 1:13-17, and John 1:1-3.)

Here's how creation happened: "Then God ___created___ " (Gen. 1:3, 6, 9, 11, 14).

> By the word of the Lord the heavens were made, and all the host of them by the breath of His mouth. (Psa. 33:6)

There was no Big Bang followed by eons of gradual evolution—not according to the Bible. God spoke and the universe appeared. Instantly. All of it. From nothing.

so that the things which are seen were not made of things which are visible.

> He has made the earth by His power; He has established the world by His wisdom, and stretched out the heaven by His understanding. (Jer. 51:15)

Your eyes can see created things. With a telescope you can study distant planets; with a microscope, infinitesimal microorganisms. But only faith can see the power and wisdom that created them all. It takes faith to believe that every visible thing was made by an invisible God—but it also takes faith (I think much more faith) to believe they crawled or sprang into existence without Him.

Scientists have gathered a vast treasury of observations of the universe. Those who believe in the God of Genesis find within that data clear evidence of an intelligent Designer Who created all things in one distinct moment in the not-so-distant past. Scientists who do not begin with belief in the Creator use the same data to work out an elaborate evolutionary timetable beginning at some imprecise moment eons ago. They fit the observable facts into a model of origins that excludes an unseeable God.

Guided by different presuppositions (belief and unbelief), these two sets of scientists use the same raw data but come to different conclusions about the beginning of the universe. Both require faith.

In elementary school we learned to do simple science projects using the scientific method. Our teachers taught us to ask a question, predict an answer, then design an *observable, repeatable* experiment to prove or disprove our theory. (This required markers, poster board, and patient parents.) Why can't any theory about the beginning of the universe be proved using the scientific method?

Since creation was not observed by humans and cannot be repeated, human theories about how it came about cannot be proved through science. They must be accepted by faith. But God was an eyewitness to creation and has told us in His Word what happened. By faith we believe what He says.

Is that blind faith or sound reason? The foundation of creationism is the unchanging written Word of God. Non-creationist concepts are theories that, though presented as truth, are uncertain and inconstant, based on the changing speculations of men. New ideas about origins are frequently doubted and discarded not long after they are presented. I have found these disclaimers in secular science textbooks, in chapters that teach about origins:

> This may explain . . .
> It's still unclear why . . .
> We are still trying to figure out how . . .
> Some scientists have suggested that . . .

There are many competing hypotheses about . . .

We do not yet have a good understanding of . . .

(And my favorite) There are many things that scientists don't know.

There are only two sources of information about the beginning of the world: God's revelation and man's theories. Both must be accepted by faith. Which do you choose?

What you believe, or do not believe, about creation matters, for it reveals who you trust to tell you the truth, and that has an impact on the rest of your life.

Faith in God's creation is the foundation of believing His Word

God first introduces us to Himself as the Creator.

> In the beginning God created the heavens and the earth. (Gen. 1:1)

> There it is. Take it or leave it. There will never be a better answer given. It is absolute, final, and true. God does not stop to explain; He is not obliged to satisfy our curiosity or stoop to satisfy man's credulity. Faith comes to rest in the first verse of the Bible, and infidelity begins right here.[1]

If Genesis 1:1 is not true, then God tells a lie in the first words of the first verse of the first chapter of the first book of the Bible. How could we trust anything that follows?

When my first child, Stephanie, began eating solid food, I read a book written by a woman known as a childhood nutrition expert. The first chapter said that the taste for sugar is acquired, not instinctive. Children don't naturally like sweets, the author said, so mothers can protect children from a lifelong craving for sugar by withholding it completely during their first years.

I believed her and did that, until the day in a friend's house when I saw my

---

[1] DeHaan, *Hebrews,* 152.

tiny girl's wildly enthusiastic reaction to her first taste of ice cream. As I tossed the book in the garbage, I believe my exact words were, "That woman's a nut!"

Maybe she wasn't actually a nut, but I had just seen the first premise in the first chapter of her book proved wrong, so I didn't trust the rest of it. If you don't believe the opening words of the Bible, what are you saying about God and His Word?

Faith in God as Creator leads to accepting Him as Savior

I introduced my children to God through creation, using simple questions like these.

> Who made the grass? (God did!)
> Who made the sun? (God did!)
> Who made you? (God did!)

(This led to a funny moment in our home when I asked our toddler Susannah, "Who made this mess?" and she happily answered, "God did!")

Children who meet God first as Creator, who grow up singing, "This Is My Father's World," often move gently toward knowing Him as Savior. But even those who missed this early training can see God in the natural world, for creation is one of the ways He reveals Himself to us.

> For since the creation of the world His invisible attributes are
> clearly seen, being understood by the things that are made, even
> His eternal power and Godhead, so that they are without excuse.
> (Rom. 1:20)

Acknowledging God as Creator is a significant step toward accepting personal responsibility for our sin against Him. When Paul was preaching to worshipers of false gods, what did he tell them about God to persuade them to turn from idols toward faith in God? (See Acts 14:15 and 17:24-25.)

During the last days (where we live now, in the years between Jesus' birth and His second coming), scoffers are especially busy denying and undermining truth. Read 2 Peter 3:3-7. According to verse 5-6, what two past acts of God do they deliberately forget?

Creation

the Flood

In the future, just before God's final wrath is poured out on the universe, He will send an angel to preach "to every nation, tribe, tongue, and people" (Rev. 14:6). All will hear one final appeal to repent and worship. What will this angel remind people about God? Why do you think He chose to emphasize that truth? (See Rev. 14:6-7.)

He created us, He has the power to judge us

False teachers have a willing and receptive audience. Why do you think most people would rather not believe in a personal Creator? Why does the devil work so hard to convince people that what the Bible says about creation is not true? *If you break down the 1st words of the Bible then you break down the rest of the word. The devil wants us to believe we are free from Gods authority.*

Faith in God's perfect creation affects your confidence in Him

If the rest of the natural universe came about by chance and random accidents, then so did you. But you didn't! You were intentionally and perfectly created, meticulously designed according to God's plan for you. Believing that He made you just right is crucial to trusting Him with everything else.

> For You formed my inward parts. You covered me in my mother's womb. (Psa. 139:13)

The organs of your body were meticulously prepared by God. He *covered* you in your mother's womb, which means He wove and knitted your parts together according to His chosen pattern. When God looks at you, He sees planned perfection. You may not think that what you see in the mirror is one bit perfect. But oh, the wonders on the inside! To look inside a human body is to be astonished at its beauty and complexity. How all your parts work in harmony—what a delicate but resilient creation you are—what an incredible Designer you have!

> I will praise You, for I am fearfully and wonderfully made. Marvelous are Your works, and that my soul knows very well. (Psa. 139:14)

If you have congenital disabilities, it can be especially hard to believe you are flawlessly created. But even without conspicuous physical defects, women are prone to criticize our bodies.

> Too short. too tall.
> Too big, too small.
> Too thin, too fat.
> Too this, too that.

That's what we think of ourselves! But no matter what your imperfections (real or imaginary), know this for certain: you are marvelously made. You are not a mistake or the haphazard outcome of conception, but the unique and perfect creation of a wise and loving God.

Your arms and legs, hands and feet, hair, skin, organs, veins, nerves, and muscles were sketched into the book of God's foreknowledge long before you were born. As an embryo in your mother's womb, you were delicately embroidered by the Master Creator. Before your parents even knew you had been conceived, you were on your way to being the woman He planned you to be.

> My frame was not hidden from You, when I was made in secret, and skillfully wrought in the lowest parts of the earth. Your eyes saw my substance, being yet unformed. And in Your book they all were written, the days fashioned for me, when as yet there were none of them. (Psa. 139:15-16)

14

You can probably imagine many upgrades to the person you see in the mirror. It's good to improve whatever you can as you try to become the best possible *you*. But what about your unwelcome but unchangeable traits? What would God say to you about them?

As you grow in faith in God as your perfect Creator, your faith will grow in other areas. You will understand how intimately He knows and loves you—just as you are. You will have confidence that even the hardest things in life are intended for your good. When you comprehend that even before you were born, He has watched over you, you will stop worrying about the future. Know that you are specially, marvelous, and perfectly created, and the rest will come easily.

Strengthen your belief in God as Creator, and your faith will grow into unshakeable confidence.

> Ah, Lord God! Behold, You have made the heavens and the earth by Your great power and outstretched arm. There is nothing too hard for You. (Jer. 32:17)

Think it through

What do you believe about the origin of all things? Why do you believe this? How has this affected your life?

CHAPTER THREE
The Sacrifice of Faith: Abel

By faith Abel offered to God a more excellent sacrifice than Cain, through which he obtained witness that he was righteous, God testifying of his gifts; and through it he being dead still speaks. (Heb. 11:4)

Does it matter what you believe, as long as you are sincere? Does it matter how you worship God, as long as you do your best? Does it matter where you put your faith, as long as it makes sense to you?

A tale of two brothers answers those crucial questions. Hebrews 11:4 introduces us to Cain and Abel. Genesis 4:1-15 fills in the details of their story, which illustrates the second thing faith does: *faith brings an acceptable sacrifice.*

Two men

The first two children born on the earth never got to live in the perfect Garden of Eden, because by the time they were born, their parents, Adam and Eve, had been evicted for disobeying their Creator. The consequences of their sin were literally earthshattering.

Perfection on the planet came to an abrupt end. God announced how things would change. Men now would have to battle thorns and thistles to raise crops for food. The struggle to survive was on. Eventually, everyone would lost that battle and die.

> In the sweat of your face you shall eat bread till you return to the ground, for out of it you were taken; for dust you are, and to dust you shall return. (Gen. 3:19)

For women, childbearing would be complicated and painful.

> I will greatly multiply your sorrow and your conception; in pain
> you shall bring forth children. (Gen. 3:16)

God also pronounced a curse on Satan, who had deceived Adam and Eve. A woman, He said, would deliver a son who, though wounded in battle with Satan, would deal him a fatal head-wound.

> I will put enmity between you and the woman, and between your
> seed [unbelievers] and her Seed [Jesus]. He shall bruise your head,
> and you shall bruise His heel. (Gen. 3:15)

How Eve must have cheered when she heard her tempter was doomed! How she must have hated that wicked one for wrecking her perfect life while pretending to be her friend.

Soon Eve had a baby, a boy. Can you imagine being the very first woman to give birth? Every labor pain must have reminded her of the curse brought by sin. But seeing her newborn son reminded her of God's promise of redemption.

When she named her baby Cain (*acquired*), she said, "I have acquired a man from the Lord" (Gen. 4:1). She knew her son was a gift from God, a sign that He still loved her. His name may also have represented Eve's hope that she had delivered the promised Seed, the One Who would destroy Satan. She could not have known it would be four thousand years before the Redeemer would arrive on earth. She did not have the privilege of being His mother, but she did become the mother of many generations who by faith watched and longed for His coming.

Finally, at just the right moment, at "the fullness of the time . . . God sent forth His Son, born of a woman, to redeem those who were under the law" (Gal. 4:4-5). The promised One had come!

Conceived in the womb of the virgin Mary through the power of the Holy Spirit, Jesus is the only child ever born without a human father—so only He can be called the Seed of a woman. Jesus lived a perfect life, then died "that through death He might destroy him who had the power of death, that is, the devil" (Heb. 2:14).

The moment Jesus rose from His tomb, the promise of Genesis 3:15 was fulfilled. The tempter's head was crushed, and his doom (though the sentence has still not been carried out) was sealed. The Seed of a woman had conquered death and broken the curse of sin. For you!

> For if by the one man's offense death reigned through the one, much more those who receive abundance of grace and of the gift of righteousness will reign in life through the One, Jesus Christ. (Rom. 5:17)

If Eve had expected Cain to be the Redeemer, she was terribly disappointed. Despite her great expectations for her son, Cain did not share his mother's relationship with God. Many mothers have known that sorrow, but this first family's catastrophe was horrific. Genesis 4:1-15 tells the tragic story of Cain and his brother Abel.

Two Offerings

What sort of work did the brothers do? (See Gen. 4:2.)

Each occupation was essential and honorable. So far, so good. But then something happened that showed how different they were. At some time, in some way, God had told Cain and Abel what He expected as an offering. What gifts did they bring? (See Gen. 4:3-4.)

How did God respond to their offerings? (See Gen. 4:4-5.)

Cain brought the first and finest produce from his garden. That was not offensive in itself. In fact, later Jews brought God their first fruits as a thanksgiving offering (Deut. 26:1-4). Cain seemed sincere, and it is likely he believed his gifts would be accepted, or he would not have brought them. So, what was the problem with Cain's worship? Was God being unreasonable, playing favorites, or showing He preferred meat to vegetables?

The One Who knows "the end from the beginning" (Isa. 46:10) had a big design in mind when He asked for specific sacrifices. The offerings were object lessons, types, and images of God's eternal plan of salvation. Every lamb on every altar from Genesis to the cross was a picture of the Lamb of God–the final, sufficient sacrifice for all sin. Bringing the precise gifts God asked for was both simple obedience and a demonstration of personal faith in One yet to come.

What is one thing all animals have that vegetables and fruits don't have?

Later God made this a requirement under the Law.

> For the life of the flesh is in the blood, and I have given it to you upon the altar to make atonement for your souls; for it is the blood that makes atonement for the soul. (Lev. 17:11)

> Without shedding of blood there is no remission. (Heb. 9:22)

Blood atonement is one of the major unifying themes of the Bible. After Adam and Eve sinned in the Garden of Eden, they were ashamed of their nakedness. God covered them with the skins of animals as a foreshadowing of the blood sacrifice that would cover our sins (Gen. 3:21.)

> Knowing that you were not redeemed with corruptible things, like
> silver or gold . . . but with the precious blood of Christ, as of a lamb
> without blemish and without spot. (1 Pet. 1:18-19)

Abel brought the sacrifice of a sinner who knew he needed redemption through blood, but Cain brought an offering that showed pride in his own accomplishments. No matter how beautiful his fruits and vegetables, no matter how good his motives, Cain's very best work could never atone for his sin.

Sincerity is not enough. We cannot bring God anything we want. We must bring what He asks for, and God asks for a blood sacrifice. We do not know how much of this symbolism the brothers understood, but they did understand obedience. Abel obeyed, but Cain did not, and that is what mattered to God.

Read Hebrews 11:4 and Matthew 23:35. What word describes Abel in both verses?

Abel was not righteous by birth, and we aren't either. When we measure ourselves by the plumb line of God's perfection, we are all hopelessly crooked. Adam's sin nature has been passed to us, so we are all born sinners. That is why it is easy for us to do wrong. It is our nature to sin.

> Therefore, just as through one man [Adam] sin entered the world,
> and death through sin, and thus death spread to all men, because
> all sinned. (Rom. 5:12)

> But we are all like an unclean thing, and all our righteousnesses
> are like filthy rags; we all fade as a leaf, and our iniquities, like the
> wind, have taken us away. (Isa. 64:6)

You cannot wash yourself clean with a filthy rag. What is the only way to be righteous? (See Phil. 3:8-9.)

Abel had the righteousness which comes by faith, but Cain did not. Because Cain was faithless, he was unrighteous. Cain was not one of God's own, but "of the wicked one." The offering he brought was not just insufficient; it was evil (1 John 3:12).

Trying to be saved by our own efforts is futile, but people keep trying. In Luke 18:9-14, Jesus told a story about a Pharisee and a tax collector. Who are they like? What did Jesus want His listeners to understand?

Cains and Pharisees live all around you. Ask your neighbors how to get to heaven, and you will probably hear some version of "believe in God, go to church, put money in the offering plate, be nice, and you'll get there." Most people think they are good people (compared to the ones who live over on the next street), so they will be in heaven with all the other good people. But goodness on the outside can never erase corruption on the inside.

> Cain was the founder of the world's first false religion, a religion which is at the heart of all false religions ever since. Essentially, Cain's religion was one of good works and human merit . . . . He offered to God the fruit of the earth, the product of his labors, the sweat of his brow, his toil and self-effort. His religion is summed up in Scripture as "the way of Cain" (Jude 11) and is rejected, root and branch, by God. It ignored Calvary and the shedding of blood.
>
> Abel, on the other hand, brought a lamb; took his stand as a hopeless sinner needing a Savior and a Substitute; and slew his lamb, shedding its blood to show his willingness to approach God in God's way.[1]

Two Destinies

In Genesis 4:6-7, God gave Cain an opportunity to make things right, to do right so he could be accepted. But Cain responded to God's lovingkindness by

---

[1] John Phillips, *Exploring Hebrews* (Chicago: Moody Bible Institute, 1977), 16

becoming a sarcastic rebel. He acted out his anger by murdering his brother, then lying to cover his crime. Rather than repenting, Cain let sin rule over him. By continuing in his rebellion, Cain showed he was a child of the devil, not a child of God. There was no faith in Cain.

> In this the children of God and the children of the devil are manifest: Whoever does not practice righteousness is not of God, nor is he who does not love his brother. For this is the message that you heard from the beginning, that we should love one another. Not as Cain who was of the wicked one and murdered his brother. And why did he murder him? Because his works were evil and his brother's righteous. (1 John 3:10-12)

The first person born on the earth was a murderer; the second was his victim. Abel was a true martyr, killed for his faith. The influence of his life has lasted long past his death. Though not a single word he said is recorded the Bible, "he being dead still speaks" (Heb. 11:4). What did God hear crying from the ground? (See Gen. 4:10).

What do you think it said? (Compare Rev. 6:9-10.)

Abel's life ended early; Cain's was long and painful. God cursed any soil Cain tried to farm, so that his crops would not grow. Cain had to live the rest of his life as a "fugitive and a vagabond," far from the God he had scorned (Gen. 4:14). Though God set a mark on him that protected him from murder, Cain still lived in constant fear of death. Wherever he went, he was a living warning of the consequences of refusing to bring the blood sacrifice God asked for. His life illustrated the tragedy of misplaced faith.

Saving faith is not simply believing that God exists; Cain was not an atheist. Saving faith is not doing good deeds; Cain brought the best he could produce. Saving faith is the absolute, exclusive reliance on Jesus as the only sufficient offering for sin. It is seeing Jesus on the cross, knowing His blood was shed for you, and by faith receiving His gift of eternal life. Faith in His completed sacrifice is the only offering God will accept.

> In whom we have redemption through his blood, the forgiveness
> of sins, according to the riches of his grace. (Eph. 1:7)

Think it through

When God looks into your heart, who does He see—Cain or Abel? What sacrifice for sin have you brought to Him?

CHAPTER FOUR
The Walk of Faith: Enoch

By faith Enoch was taken away so that he did not see death, and was not found,
because God had taken him; for before he was taken he had this testimony,
that he pleased God. But without faith it is impossible to please Him, for he
who comes to God must believe that He is, and that He is a rewarder of
those who diligently seek Him. (Heb. 11:5-6)

Do you want to please God? Live like Enoch! Enoch's life teaches us that *faith walks with God.*

Enoch was born into the seventh generation after Adam. His name is buried in the long list of short obituaries in Genesis 5:1-32. Most of these epitaphs are rather ordinary, but Enoch's is special.

> So all the days of Enoch were three hundred and sixty-five years.
> And Enoch walked with God; and he was not, for God took him.
> (Gen. 5:23-24)

One thing is obvious: people were obeying God's command to "be fruitful and multiply" (Gen. 1:28). They were also dying, just as He had said they would. "And he died" is true of everybody in the Genesis 5 list—except Enoch. After a lifetime of walking with God, Enoch skipped death to walk right into eternity. He simply *was* and then he *wasn't.*

Though he lived to be 365, Enoch's life was short, relative to his relatives. His son Methuselah lived to be 969! But Enoch lived an exemplary life. During a time when few other people lived righteously, what did Enoch do? (See Gen. 5:22, 24.)

The faith Enoch models for us is vigorous, not sedentary. Faith takes action!

Walking by faith calls for making a choice

To walk with God means to walk in step with Him, to match strides with Him by continuously, consciously yielding your will to His, moving in any direction He chooses. That is what Jesus did, and He's our model.

> For I have come down from heaven, not to do My own will, but the will of Him who sent Me. (John 6:38)
>
> He who says he abides in Him ought himself also to walk just as He walked. (1 John 2:6)

Enoch walked in step with God for three hundred years (Gen. 5:22). That is amazing to me because I find it impossible to live even one day in unspoiled companionship with Him. I like to do things my own way, and that never ends well. I hide from God like Adam and Eve in the Garden. Sin always ruins fellowship with God.

My natural way is ugly. What is the fleshly walk like? (See Eph. 4:17-19.)

What is the opposite of walking in the flesh? (See Gal. 5:16.)

People who walk in the Spirit cannot walk in step with those who walk in the flesh. Our pace and direction are so different that our paths naturally diverge.

> Can two walk together, unless they are agreed [in harmony]? (Amos 3:3)

If you want to walk with God, how should you relate to those who don't? (See 2 Cor. 6:14-18.)

Walking by faith calls for courage

Enoch was a bold prophet who confronted sinners through fiery sermons.

> Now Enoch, the seventh from Adam, prophesied about these men also, saying, "Behold, the Lord comes with ten thousands of His saints, to execute judgment on all, to convict all who are ungodly among them of all their ungodly deeds which they have committed in an ungodly way, and of all the harsh things which ungodly sinners have spoken against Him." (Jude 14-15)

The Lord, Enoch declared, would someday come with a congregation of His saints to test and convict all the *ungodly* of all their *ungodly* works which they did in an *ungodly* way, and of the harsh words spoken by the *ungodly* against God.

Jude could have used a thesaurus! But what better word is there than *ungodly* to sum up the behavior of the wicked? Remember that Enoch was not preaching to the church choir but to the profane, corrupt, depraved, vile people living on earth before the flood—faithless people who had "gone in the way of Cain" (Jude 11).

I am glad God has not called me to preach like Enoch. I would be terrified. Or maybe I just don't have his faith. What gave Enoch the confidence to boldly forecast future judgment? Why does a prophet have to preach "by faith, not by sight" (2 Cor. 5:7)?

Enoch's prophecy will be completely fulfilled when Jesus, accompanied by His saints, arrives for the final judgment (2 Thess. 1:7-9 & 1 Cor. 6:2-3). Maybe Enoch will appear as one of the people in that great congregation of saints. Though this judgment is still in the future, the earth has already seen a sampling of God's judgment—the worldwide flood of Noah's day.

Like his great-grandfather Enoch, Noah was a righteous man living in an ungodly world (Gen. 6:8-12). But even while living in societies saturated with wickedness, Enoch and Noah walked with God. Because they saw the future with eyes of faith, they were able to preach truth boldly, fearlessly warning sinners of coming judgment. Their faith gave substance to their vision, and that gave them confidence.

We believe what the Bible says about the horrors of hell, but it's hard to tell our unsaved friends what awaits the lost. I would rather please people than provoke them, wouldn't you? The only way to reduce your fear of confrontation and rejection is to increase your faith. As faith grows, so does boldness with hard truths.

Walking by faith calls for knowing God

To walk with God like Enoch, you must by faith believe that . . .

He is

God's Word does not attempt to prove He is real. It just says, "In the beginning, God" (Gen. 1:1). The eternal, self-existent One has no need to convince us He is alive. There is a powerful majesty to God's statements about Himself. He simply tells us that He exists, and that He is the only true and living Deity.

> And God said to Moses, "I am Who I am." (Exod. 3:14)

> I am God, and there is no other; I am God, and there is none like Me. (Isa. 46:9)

But God does reveal Himself to us. He appears on every page of the Bible, which is now more easily and widely available than ever.

> You search the Scriptures . . . these are they which testify of Me. (John 5:39)

He also shows Himself through nature, which daily points our thoughts toward a Designer and Sustainer.

> For since the creation of the world His invisible attributes are clearly seen, being understood by the things that are made, even His eternal power and Godhead, so that they are without excuse. (Rom. 1:20)

And He speaks quietly through the conscience, with its innate capacity to feel guilt and the need of forgiveness.

> For when Gentiles, who do not have the law, by nature do the things in the law, these, although not having the law, are a law to themselves, who show the work of the law written in their hearts, their conscience also bearing witness, and between themselves their thoughts accusing or else excusing them. (Rom. 2:14-15)

These compasses point us toward God, but it is only by faith that we can know He *is*. Unbelievers need faith, too—faith in their own minds.

Our family had a friend who was an ardent unbeliever. We liked him and admired his professional accomplishments. He was a genuinely hospitable and generous man, and since whatever we believed, he believed the opposite, dinner conversations at his house were never dull.

He had read and studied the Bible, not to understand, but to criticize. He was disdainful of believers as intellectually deficient and was defiant toward the God he claimed didn't exist. We knew there was no way we could by reason or logic prove God's existence or argue our friend into believing, so we just asked God to do His convicting work in our friend's heart.

Before he died, we saw one tiny softening of his spirit. We were talking with him about our visit to a national monument near his home, a place where thousand-year old redwood trees soar toward heaven in a setting that inspires reverence and worship for the Creator.

Our friend said, "Yes, that is a beautiful place," then continued quietly, "When I'm there, I look up at those trees and wonder if ... just maybe ... I might be wrong about God."

God spoke to him through creation, and his conscience was stirred. But as far as we know, our friend never responded to Him in faith. Trusting his own reason kept him from trusting God.

He rewards those who diligently seek Him

God does not play "hide and seek" with us. Anyone who looks for Him will find Him.

> I love those who love me, and those who seek me diligently will find me. (Prov. 8:17)

Seeking God may be as simple as getting up early to soak in His Word or sacrificing other enjoyable but less-important pursuits to spend time with Him. A faith-fueled passion to know God will always be rewarded; a search for Him will never hit a dead end. God promises that as you move toward Him, He will move toward you (James 4:8).

It may be hard to believe that with 7.7 billion people on this planet, God would notice you—but He does. He wants to walk with you as much as if you were the only person on earth.

> Then you will call upon Me and go and pray to Me, and I will listen to you. And you will seek Me and find Me, when you search for Me with all your heart. I will be found by you, says the Lord. (Jer. 29:12-14)

Even in our own "present evil age" (Gal. 1:4), you and I can stay as close to God as Enoch was. We can walk in the Spirit rather than in the flesh; we can walk with courage; by faith we can know that He is real and that we have truly found Him as our Savior.

Think it through

Think back over the last few days. Did you consistently walk in step with God? Were you courageous with His truth? Did you actively seek Him? What should you do differently tomorrow?

CHAPTER FIVE
The Impossibles of Faith: Noah

> By faith Noah, being divinely warned of things not yet seen, moved
> with godly fear, prepared an ark for the saving of his household, by
> which he condemned the world and became heir of the righteousness
> which is according to faith. (Heb 11:7)

Noah and the ark—we rarely speak of one without the other. But it would be better to link Noah with faith, for the ark stood (and floated) as a symbol of his extraordinary trust in God. Noah's life illustrates the next thing faith does: *faith does the impossible.*

Noah's father Lamech gave his son a name meaning *rest,* hoping that "this one will comfort us concerning our work and the toil of our hands, because of the ground which the Lord has cursed" (Gen. 5:29). Lamech was already an old man and glad to have a son to help with the sweaty grind of farming. He could not have known that Noah would be unique among all the people on earth or that his son would play such a significant role in the planet's transformation.

A wicked world

When the Lord looked at the earth before the flood, what did He see? (See Gen. 6:5, 11-12.)

a corrupt & evil world

Why did people act that way? (See Matt. 15:18-19.)

they had evil hearts

We use the word "inhumane" to describe something especially cruel or vicious. But humans are capable of ruthless brutality. Genesis 6 recounts how God felt about what He saw on the earth and what He decided to do about it.

> And the Lord was sorry that He had made man on the earth, and He was grieved in His heart. So the Lord said, "I will destroy man whom I have created from the face of the earth, both man and beast, creeping thing and birds of the air, for I am sorry that I have made them.
>
> And God said to Noah, "The end of all flesh has come before Me, for the earth is filled with violence through them; and behold, I will destroy them with the earth.
>
> "And behold, I Myself am bringing floodwaters on the earth, to destroy from under heaven all flesh in which is the breath of life; everything that is on the earth shall die." (Gen. 6:6-7, 13, 17)

It would be understandable if God regretted creating people. Since Adam and Eve's sin, life on this planet had quickly and steadily deteriorated. Was God caught off guard by human rebellion and compelled to come up with a Plan B? That doesn't sound like the God we know, the One Whose plans never go awry.

Long before the Garden, long before the flood, God knew His creatures would fill the earth with wickedness. Though sad and displeased by what they had done, He was not surprised. The God Who "works all things according to the counsel of His will" (Eph. 1:11) always knows what is ahead, for He planned it all.

> For I am God, and there is no other; I am God, and there is none like Me, declaring the end from the beginning, and from ancient times things that are not yet done, saying, "My counsel shall stand, and I will do all My pleasure." (Isaiah 46:9-10)

A righteous man

In Genesis 6:9, we meet Noah, a one-of-a-kind man. He "was a ___just___ man, _perfect_ in his _generations_ blameless compared to his contemporaries. Nobody is sinless, but Noah was genuinely devoted and absolutely faithful to God. In the middle of a world engulfed by wickedness, Noah walked with God. That is an even greater accomplishment than building an ark.

> For the grace of God that brings salvation has appeared to all men, teaching us that, denying ungodliness and worldly lusts, we should live soberly, righteously, and godly in the present age. (Titus 2:11-12)

Noah had godly fear. To fear God does not mean to be terrified of Him but to feel reverence and awe toward Him. Do you fear God? How does that change the way you live?

An impossible assignment

God warned Noah that the end of the world as he knew it was near. All people, along with land-dwelling animals and birds, would die in a universal flood. Noah's assignment was to build a floating vessel to preserve seeds of human and animal life to repopulate earth.

God gave Noah blueprints for constructing an enormous box with three decks of cabin-like rooms, made of gopher wood (cedar or cypress) and covered with pitch for waterproofing. In our measurements, the ark was 510 feet long, 85 feet wide, and 51 feet high—about the same size and with the same stability as a modern cargo vessel.

Construction of the ark took 120 years. I really do hope Noah's family helped him—but the job was specifically his. To have courage to even begin building the ark, Noah had to believe in what had never been seen before: enough water falling from the sky and gushing from below the earth's surface to completely cover the globe. And he had to have faith that the God-designed, never-before-seen lifeboat he was building would actually float.

God told Noah the flood would come; Noah believed Him and built. He listened and did *exactly* what God said to do. Noah obeyed the impossible commands of an invisible Being. That's faith.

> Thus Noah did; according to all that God commanded him, so he did. (Gen. 6:22)

For over a century, Noah sawed, hammered, and spread pitch over this monstrous wooden monument to his faith. But Noah wasn't just a boat-builder. What else was he? (See 2 Pet. 2:5.)

preacher of righteousness

Imagine Noah pausing from his work to stand on a partially completed deck of the ark to preach to a gawking, mocking crowd. What would Noah have said to them?

Noah didn't know when the rains would start. He just worked until the work was done and preached as he worked. Read Genesis 6:19-21. What were Noah's other tasks?

caretaker
cleaner
captain, etc.

When the animals arrived, the ark was ready for them. Noah had set up living quarters for his family of eight, stocked with all they would need for a long sea voyage. He had prepared the rest of the huge space inside the ark as a floating zoo equipped with enough bedding, food, and water for two (and in some cases seven) of every species of animal, bird, and creeping thing.

Noah did not have to locate, lasso, trap, capture, and herd the animals into the ark. God sent them. Noah had prepared the space with faith that the impossible would happen: a horde of walking, crawling, hopping, slithering, and flying creatures would arrive on time and willingly, peacefully settle into their homes.

That took faith—not only in what *he* had never seen, but in what *no one* had ever seen. No dark storm clouds had yet started gathering on the horizon; no warning rumbles were coming from the fountains of the deep. Noah trusted the word of a God he had never seen.

A divine plan

<u>Judgment of the wicked</u>

The world before the flood was thoroughly rotten. Before it drowned in water, it had already drowned in sin. For 120 years, "the Divine longsuffering waited . . . while the ark was being prepared" (1 Pet. 3:20). Noah's constant warnings "condemned the world" (Heb. 11:7) who heard them but did not respond in faith. It must have been discouraging to Noah when not a single person outside his immediate family responded to his warnings. The people who heard him were blinded by their sin and distracted by the routines and indulgences of life.

> For as in the days before the flood, they were eating and drinking, marrying and giving in marriage, until the day that Noah entered the ark, and did not know until the flood came and took them all away. (Matt. 24:38-39)

Some heard Noah preach and walked away laughing. *What a nut. Not even God (if He even exists) could kill us all at once. Never happened before. Never will happen. Ridiculous. Impossible.*

Others listened without mocking. *It's possible. But not likely, at least not anytime soon. We're no worse than anybody else. In fact, we're better than most.*

Others listened more thoughtfully. *Noah is right. We are sinners, and God is angry with us. But surely there's a more dignified way to escape. The monstrosity that eccentric man calls a boat is just too weird.*

Others heard, then came back to hear more, thinking seriously about what Noah said. They were alarmed when they saw animals arriving in pairs but quickly dismissed their anxieties. *It's probably just some new migration pattern. We will figure it out later when we are not so busy.*

When God called time, Noah, his wife, and his three sons and their wives joined the animals on the ark. God Himself shut the door. Then . . . nothing happened. The family settled in, fed and watered the animals, and waited. Maybe they heard sporadic laughter coming from outside or an occasional tentative knock on the door.

Suddenly the windows of heaven opened, and the fountains of waters stored under the earth broke loose. Churning water seeped under the doors of houses and inched up their walls. Floodwaters covered rooftops and chased families up mountainsides. Drowning animals bellowed and squealed. Doomed souls screamed in terror and begged Noah to let them in.

We have made the tale of Noah's flood a bedtime story for children, but in reality, it was horrible.

<u>Salvation of the righteous</u>

Among the drowning there surely were some who had believed the flood was going to come but were not willing to climb on board. What is the difference between Noah's faith and theirs? Find the answer in James 2:14-26.

We know Noah's family's faith was real because of what they *did:* they got on board! They were not saved by climbing the ramp into the ark but by the faith that motivated their steps. The faith that saves moves a sinner to *do* something.

The ark had only one door. Salvation has only one door, Jesus Christ. We are not saved when we believe the door is open for us, but when we walk through it, by faith.

I am the door. If anyone enters by Me, he will be saved. (John 10:9)

My husband David's salvation testimony illustrates the difference between knowing the truth and acting in faith.

> I grew up in a Christian home, so involved in church that I attended Sunday school for nine years in a row without missing a Sunday. I was a good kid and, even in the 60s, not a rebel.
>
> As a student at a Christian college, I had no assurance I was saved. I tried to dismiss my doubts, arguing with myself: "C'mon, Dave, you're okay. You've believed in Christ all your life. Don't be one of those unstable guys who 'gets saved' over and over."
>
> Hoping to find peace in my heart, I changed my major from cinema to Christian education and spent a summer working at a Christian camp. When I applied to join a summer mission to New York City, the team leader asked me when I was saved.
>
> "I'm not sure of the exact date," I answered. "But I think I did it when I was a kid."
>
> He answered, "You may not know the exact day you received Christ as Savior. But if you don't at least know the year you made the most important decision of your life, you may always doubt your salvation."
>
> Then my friend read Romans 8:16: "The Spirit Himself bears witness with our spirit that we are children of God." I prayed and asked God to tell me if I was really saved, and immediately I knew I wasn't.
>
> I had intellectually agreed with the truths of salvation but had never

personally admitted my sin and trusted Christ. My "salvation" had been a collective agreement with my parents, church, and friends. I dropped to my knees and prayed, admitting I was a sinner and asking Jesus to save my soul.

When I got up from my knees, I knew I was a born-again Christian!

David was not saved by what he knew. He was saved when he entered salvation's door.

Noah and his family spent months afloat. There was plenty to do, of course, with so many creatures to feed and clean up after. But the days were long, and God had not told them when the flood would end. Think of the stamina they needed, the courage to endure, the patience to wait for the end of their isolation.

Finally, the rain stopped. A strong wind passed over and the waters receded. Oceans deepened and mountains rose, transforming the earth. The ark perched on a high peak. When a dove flew away from the ark and returned with a green leaf, hopes rose.

Finally, after a year on board the ark, the eight people still alive on earth stepped with wobbly legs onto dry ground. Noah built an altar and sacrificed the clean animals preserved especially for this moment. As the rest of the creatures scattered, Noah's family worshiped and praised God for life.

One of the lessons of Noah's story is that the Creator of the physical universe is not limited by its laws; the Creator of people is not bound by their will. He can do the impossible. What does God look for in us before doing miracles for us? (See Matt. 17:20, Mark 9:23.)

The family was told to "be fruitful and multiply, and fill the earth" (Gen. 9:1). They did, and through this one family "the whole earth was populated" (Gen. 9:19). Noah is the common ancestor of us all, so you share his DNA. Do you also share his faith—the faith that accomplishes the impossible?

Think it through

Recall a time when you faced an impossible task. Did you start well, press on, and have success? Did you start, get discouraged by opposition, and quit? Or were you too scared to even try? What made the difference?

CHAPTER SIX
The Qualities of Genuine Faith: Abraham
Part One

> By faith Abraham obeyed when he was called to go out to the place
> which he would receive as an inheritance. And he went out, not
> knowing where he was going. (Heb. 11:8)

Abraham did something strange—packed up his family, belongings, and
beasts and set out on an extended, open-ended trip, with no idea where he
was going. Abraham was not being irrational, rash, reckless, or foolhardy. He
was simply by faith doing what God told Him to do. Here are three more
things faith does: *faith listens to God, obeys Him, and separates from the world.*

Abraham was born about three centuries after the flood. By that time, Noah's
descendants had spread across the globe and once more were defying and
denying God's authority over them. It's sad but not surprising, for all are
sinners.

> As it is written: "There is none righteous, no, not one; there is
> none who understands; there is none who seeks after God. They
> have all turned aside; they have together become unprofitable;
> there is none who does good, no, not one." (Rom. 3:10-12)

The flood had transformed the geography of the earth but not the sinful
hearts of the people living on it. They needed a Savior. Abraham's life was
pivotal in God's plan to send that One. Jesus was born into the family line
fathered by Abraham.

Two groups can rightfully call Abraham their father. He is the physical
ancestor of the Jews, and he is also the spiritual father of Gentiles who believe
in Abraham's God. Not all fathers are good examples (and Abraham certainly

was not perfect), but when it comes to faith, you cannot find a better model than Abraham. You can take God's word for it: Abraham's faith was real.

> He believed in the Lord, and He accounted it to him for righteousness. (Gen. 15:6)

God saw Abraham's genuine faith and listed him in His ledger in the *RIGHTEOUS* column. Let's see what Father Abraham's faith was like, so we can imitate him and be "blessed with believing Abraham" (Gal. 3:9).

Genuine faith listens to God

We are first introduced to Abraham in Genesis 11:26, near the end of the genealogy of Noah's son Shem. Here he's called "Abram." Later, God changed his name to Abraham and his wife Sarai's name to Sarah. We will use those later names now since they are the ones we're most familiar with.

Abraham's family lived in Ur—a large, prosperous, wicked city located on the fertile plain of Shinar, between the Tigris and Euphrates Rivers. What does Joshua 24:2 tell us about Abraham's father, Terah?

He served other gods

Abraham was almost certainly an idol worshiper like his father. If his story had ended there, *Abraham* would be just another name in a long list of forgotten people. But what extraordinary thing happened to this otherwise ordinary man? (See Acts 7:2-3.)

God spoke to him & told him to leave

We do not know how God's voice sounded, but when Abraham heard it, he knew He was hearing from the one true and living God. I have often wished God would speak to me out loud like that. Haven't you? But you and I have resources better than anything Abraham could have imagined.

The first is the Word of God. Abraham had no written scriptures, so to hear from God he had to wait for Him to appear in person. Anytime we want to hear from God, all we have to do is open the Bible and read. Sometimes He speaks to us through His Word in a remarkably personal way.

My husband and I were on a long drive through a cold rain, on our way to spend a few days in ministry together. We were going through a heart-crushing trial. The pain was sharp, the ache relentless, and the doubt deep.

For the next two days I was going to be speaking to women who needed to hear words of confident trust in the God Who does all things well. But my faith tank was empty, and I had little to offer. Nothing, really. A storm was raging in my soul, and all I wanted to do was go home, hide under the covers, and cry.

The day grew dusky-dark and we got hungry. I wanted to do a quick drive-through-grab-and-go for dinner, mostly so I wouldn't have to talk, even to a waitress. But David had heard of a small-town restaurant along the way that served warm homestyle meals prepared by an Amish family, and he thought that was what we both needed.

He was right. It was a gentle place, welcoming and nourishing, with smiles, soft rolls, and creamy coffee. It helped. I even felt like visiting the attached gift shop before heading back out into the damp cold. After just a few minutes of wandering, though, despair came back. In a rush. Tears welled and my knees wobbled. I headed toward a wooden rocker in a corner, sat down, closed my eyes, and talked to God.

When I opened my eyes, I found myself literally surrounded by truth. All around me in that section of the shop, God's promises—painted, printed, embossed, and embroidered—covered every inch from wall to wall and floor to ceiling. I whispered those scriptures to myself, every one of them, and felt them sink down into my soul.

When I got up from that chair, my faith tank had been filled by the living Word of God. Our storm was not over yet. In fact, it soon got a little worse, but the peace I found that day lasted till it ended. No more panic. The Word of God had done its work in me.

If your faith is feeble today, find a comfortable chair, take a seat, and open God's Book. Feed on its words and see what happens.[1]

Another amazing gift we have that Abraham did not have is the continuous presence of the Holy Spirit. The Spirit does not come and go as He did in Old Testament days when He gave selected people temporary power for specific tasks. The moment you were saved, He moved in to live with you. Whenever you need Him, He's there.

> The Spirit of truth, whom the world cannot receive, because it neither sees Him nor knows Him; but you know Him, for He dwells with you and will be in you. (John 14:17)

> But the Helper, the Holy Spirit, whom the Father will send in My name, He will teach you all things, and bring to your remembrance all things that I said to you. (John 14:26)

Abraham heard God's voice. So can you! Open the Word, ask the Holy Spirit to speak to you, and "your ears shall hear a word behind you, saying, 'This is the way, walk in it'" (Isa. 30:21).

Genuine faith obeys God

At first, Abraham and his family settled in Haran, where the Lord repeated His command and added new promises. Here is the basic outline of what we now call the Abrahamic Covenant. As time passed, God gradually expanded it.

> <u>The command</u>
> Now the Lord had said to Abram: "Get out of your country, from your family and from your father's house, to a land that I will show you.

---

[1] Excerpt from Claudia Barba, "Walking on the Water," *Frontline,* Nov.-Dec. 2020, 35.

The promises

"I will make you a great nation; I will bless you and make your name great; and you shall be a blessing. I will bless those who bless you, and I will curse him who curses you; and in you all the families of the earth shall be blessed." (Gen. 12:1-3)

If God spoke to you this this, you would know Who you were hearing from. If He asked you to serve Him in an unfamiliar place, it would be a place you could find on Google maps and research on the internet. But Abraham was hearing a voice nobody else heard, coming from a God no one (including him) had ever seen, asking him to abandon his settled life to travel in an unspecified direction to an unknown place. And Abraham obeyed. That is faith.

Imagine Abraham's conversations with his family and neighbors, and especially with Sarah.

We're moving.

Where?
I don't know.

Why?
I heard a voice that told me to go.

Whose voice?
God's.

Which god?
The one and only God.

Which way are we going?
I don't know. He will lead us.

Where will we live?
In the land He promises to give us.

What will we do there?
Build a great nation.

Why?
He wants to make my name great and through me bless all the families of the earth, forever.

Have you lost your mind?

Abraham must have faced disbelief and disapproval, but he went anyway. He must have been told he was acting like a fool, but he went anyway. Step by step, not knowing where he was going, he went. Like Noah, Abraham had the kind of faith that simply hears and obeys.

And Abraham obeyed quickly. The Greek verb tenses in Hebrews 11:8 indicate that Abraham obeyed before God's voice faded away. One day Abraham was a pagan living in a settled land; the next he was a believer in Jehovah, with his face set toward the unknown.

Abraham led the way as his family, servants, and animals followed God's gradual leading. They had no map, no information about the terrain, and no human guide who knew what was ahead. While they camped by a landmark tree near Shechem, God talked to Abraham again and expanded His covenant promises. Who else was now included? (See Gen. 12:7.)

his seed

How did Abraham respond? (See Gen. 12:7-8.)

built an altar

This is the first time anyone worshiped and prayed to Jehovah in the land of promise, but since that day, Canaan has been the center and focus of God's work of redemption.

God did not entice Abraham with an offer of free land as a reward if he would obey and go. Abraham obeyed and went because He believed God's promise that the land was already his. What special relationship does God have with people with that kind of obedient faith? (See James 2:23 and John 15:14.)

Does God call you His friend?

Genuine faith separates from the world

To follow God, Abraham had to leave behind the familiar patterns of his life. The life of faith is often uncomfortable, for it calls for resting in God alone rather than other sources of security. Abraham left his old, dead idols for a new and living God, "the Lord, God Most High, the Possessor of heaven and earth" (Gen. 14:22). He left a comfortable home to live in tents in a foreign country, where the only guarantee was the presence of God. Since Abraham wanted God more than comfort, he was willing to obey, even if that brought personal loss. God, not anyone or anything else, was His security. That is faith.

A missionary couple in a foreign country wrote this during the COVID pandemic.

> *While life now seems uncertain, we are reminded that nothing is ever sure and secure except what God says and wills to be so. Although we have not yet been exposed to the virus, it has revealed our sense of addiction to comfort and control and exposed what's really in our soul.*

Maybe it is exposing the gods we worship: our health, our hurry, and our security. Now that the Lord has removed many of the attractions and distractions that once replaced Him in our lives, may we take this time to humble ourselves, pray, and seek His face. God is more than enough and all that we need!

When you accepted Jesus as your Savior, you took your first step of separation from the world. You went from the darkness of sin to the light of the gospel; you "turned to God from idols to serve the living and true God" (1 Thess. 1:9). By faith, you followed your new King from the old life to the new. Everything changed!

> He has delivered us from the power of darkness and conveyed us into the kingdom of the Son of His love. (Col. 1:13)

What did Jesus ask His disciples to do? (See Matt. 10:37-39.)

follow and love him above all else

What does a growing Christian leave behind?

Matthew 6:19, 24—

treasures upon earth , money
~~not charity we~~

Ephesians 4:22-31—

Our old (hateful, angry, bitter) speech, corruption
anything that does not glorify God , attitudes

Colossians 3:8—

anger, wrath, malice, filthy communication,
blasphemy

1 Peter 2:1—

malice, guile, hypocrisies, envies, evil speakings

For the rest of his earthly life, Abraham had no permanent home, even in the land of promise. The field of Machpelah, bought to use as a family cemetery, was the only property he ever owned in the land (Gen. 23:17-20). God gave Abraham the land, but his descendants received the title deed.

People with faith like Abraham's don't mind living like nomads with goatskin tents. They say, "Here we have no continuing city, but we seek the one to come" (Heb. 13:14). If you live for heaven, how will your life on earth look?

Think it through

What things of the world have you separated from since you were saved? What do you still need to separate from?

CHAPTER SEVEN
The Qualities of Genuine Faith: Abraham
Part Two

By faith Sarah herself also received strength to conceive seed, and she bore a child when she was past the age, because she judged Him faithful who had promised. Therefore from one man, and him as good as dead, were born as many as the stars of the sky in multitude—innumerable as the sand which is by the seashore. (Heb. 11:11-12)

By faith Abraham, when he was tested, offered up Isaac, and he who had received the promises offered up his only begotten son, of whom it was said, "In Isaac your seed shall be called," concluding that God was able to raise him up, even from the dead, from which he also received him in a figurative sense. (Heb. 11:17-19)

Genuine faith like Abraham's listens, obeys, and sacrifices, and more: *faith waits, and faith passes the test.*

Faith waits

Abraham's family were nomadic shepherds with large flocks. During a conflict over grazing space, Lot separated from his uncle Abraham and moved his family onto the best land. God saw Abraham's hurt and came to encourage His friend. What two legacies did He remind Abraham were his? (See Gen. 13:14-17.)

Look in all directions. Walk the length and width of this land. It's yours! You're going to need lots of space, because your descendants will be as countless as the dust of the earth.

At that time, Abraham and Sarah had no children at all. Abraham must have expected his wife to start having babies right away, one after another, two or three at a time! But she didn't. Years came and went, but no babies arrived in their tent. Not even one.

I am sure Abraham's faith was a bit shaken, and he wondered what was going on. He even complained to God. *How can I be the father of a multitude if I don't have even one child? I'm getting older by the day. I have even had to choose a servant to be my heir.*

Again, God came to reassure Abraham. "Look now toward heaven, and count the stars if you are able to number them. . . . So shall your descendants be" (Gen. 15:5). Then He used a strange ancient ceremony to demonstrate that His promises were unconditional. In those days, when two people made a covenant that required them both to keep their word, as a symbol of commitment they would cut an animal in half and together walk between the pieces.

But God put Abraham to sleep and "like a smoking oven and a burning torch" passed alone between the split carcasses of a heifer, goat, ram, turtledove, and pigeon (Gen. 15:17). God was putting Himself under solitary obligation to fulfill His covenant with Abraham. And God never, ever breaks His word.

> God is not a man, that He should lie, nor a son of man, that He should repent. Has He said, and will He not do? Or has He spoken, and will He not make it good? (Num. 23:19)

Soon Abraham reached his mid-eighties. Hope was fading. Month after month, Sarah waited and hoped to conceive but remained childless. In her world, barrenness was a misfortune—even a shame. The wait for the promised son seemed interminable. Weak in faith, knowing there was no natural way she and Abraham could conceive, Sarah lost patience.

So she turned to a custom of the pagan women around her: offering a maidservant to your husband as a surrogate to give birth to his heir. Sarah chose Hagar. Read the story in Genesis 16:1-16.

When Abraham agreed with Sarah's plan, it was a huge lapse of faith, one that has had major spiritual and political consequences ever since. Ishmael, the son born to Abraham through Hagar, became the father of the Arabs, the fierce and perpetual enemy of Abraham's other descendants, the Jews. The continuing conflict between Arabs and Jews is in the news every day. But despite Abraham's failure, God's plan was still in place because it was unconditional. Read Genesis 17:1-22.

This time when God repeated His promises, He gave more specifics. How long would the covenant last? So who still rightfully owns the land of Canaan? (See Gen. 17:7-8.)

God also established circumcision as a physical sign of His covenant with the Jews (Gen. 17:10-14) and for the first time, told Abraham who would bear the son of promise. In a year, Sarah would give birth to a boy. How old were Abraham and Sarah when they heard that news? (See Gen. 17:17, 24.)

No wonder Abraham laughed! Thirteen years had passed since God had last reminded Abraham of the promised heir. Sarah was now long past her fertile years, and as far as fathering a child goes, Abraham was "as good as dead" (Heb. 11:12). Compare Genesis 12:4 to Genesis 21:5. How many years after leaving Haran for the Promised Land was Isaac born to Abraham and Sarah?

When God's delay seems endless, shallow faith can be shattered. But steadfast faith grows in confidence in the God who never changes, the One who never breaks His Word.

> Heaven and earth will pass away, but My words will by no means pass away. (Luke 21:33)

A relative of mine wrote this just before a milestone birthday, during a long stretch of faith-testing suffering.

> *When we experience trials—sickness, the betrayal or death of a loved one, financial devastation, the loss of a career—it can be difficult to move forward again with the same faith we might have had in our youth. The longer our hopes are deferred, the easier it is for our hearts to grow sick (Prov. 13:12). Especially if our bodies are older, our capacities are changed, or the circumstances around us have moved on, we are prone to wonder if God can raise anything beautiful from the ashes.*
>
> *In times like these, passages like Psalm 107 draw our focus with the lighthouse-beam of God's changeless character. Whatever else goes on in our lives, this will always remain true of Jehovah: "Oh, give thanks to the Lord, for He is good! For His mercy endures forever!" (v. 1).*
>
> *No matter our age or circumstance, it should be easy to trust that the One Who spoke everything from nothing can bring something beautiful from the ashes. Though our lives may have changed, He and His love for us have not—and will not. He is the wellspring of our faith for the future, whatever He may ordain. When I ponder that, my heart joins the refrain of Psalm 107: "Oh, that men would give thanks to the Lord, for His goodness, and for His wonderful works to the children of men!" (v. 8).*

God is faithful, even to His impatient, imperfect children like Sarah and me. And you!

> The Lord visited Sarah as He had said, and the Lord did for Sarah as He had spoken. For Sarah conceived and bore Abraham a son in his old age, at the set time of which God had spoken to him. And Abraham called the name of his son who was born to him—whom Sarah bore to him—Isaac. (Gen. 21:1-3)

In Hebrews 11:11, Sarah is honored for her faith, flawed as it was. Her faith was inseparable from Abraham's, since for Isaac to be born, they needed to be joined in both body and spirit. Though the promises were made directly to Abraham, Sarah shared in his blessings and honor.

Obviously, these were fallible folks. But God graciously praised the triumph of their trust. Only genuine faith could survive such a long wait.

> And not being weak in faith, he [Abraham] did not consider his own body, already dead (since he was about a hundred years old), and the deadness of Sarah's womb. He did not waver at the promise of God through unbelief, but was strengthened in faith, giving glory to God, and being fully convinced that what He had promised He was also able to perform. And therefore "it was accounted to him for righteousness." (Rom. 4:19-22)

Faith passes the test

By faith Abraham had left home for the unknown. By faith he had fathered a miracle child. By faith he had listened, obeyed, separated, and waited. But God was still growing Abraham's faith. Until we are safely home, God never stops teaching us, as a pastor friend reminded me: "Faith knows that God's provision of one need will often be followed by a new need, and that's okay. God will eventually meet that need as well. He does not grow weary. Faith recognizes that the classroom of faith has a lifetime enrollment. We don't graduate from it in a year."

In Genesis 22:1-19, God sent Abraham his toughest test yet.

> Then He said, "Take now your son, your only son Isaac, whom you love, and go to the land of Moriah, and offer him there as a burnt offering on one of the mountains of which I shall tell you." (Gen. 22:2)

Ask a father to kill his son? It's unthinkable. And this was no ordinary son. It was Abraham's *only* son. Or was he? Wasn't Ishmael Abraham's son, too? Read Genesis 17:18-21, and you'll understand what God meant. Ishmael was Abraham's son, but not his heir. Isaac was the chosen heir of God's covenant promises, so he was irreplaceable. Without Isaac, the promises God made to Abraham meant nothing; they could not be fulfilled.

Isaac was also the son Abraham *loved*. Why do you think God mentioned that just before asking Abraham to kill him?

Watching your child suffer in any way stretches faith to the breaking point, especially when it seems that God is ignoring your desperate prayers. God knew Abraham would find it almost impossibly hard to hurt his beloved Isaac. God knows that when your child hurts, you hurt too.

These words came from the heart of a mother facing the possibility that her little girl would not recover from a critical illness. Her faith was severely tested.

> *Sometimes life gets dark. Really, really dark.*
>
> *A few days ago, we felt so low, and that everything about our situation was only getting darker. And though we clung to truth with mustard seed faith, we felt abandoned by God. We know deeply that is not true. But we felt that way.*
>
> *Our daughter has been so sick and in so much pain. We have no answers, no light at the end of the tunnel. As I came back into her room one night to face hours of moving/adjusting my girl to help the pain and make her comfortable enough to sleep, I told God I had only the tiniest bit of faith left.*
>
> *And in that dark room, in such a dark valley, Jesus reminded me that He had faced complete darkness on the cross. Because He loved me. And He actually was abandoned, as God the Father turned His back.*
>
> *And as I cried for the pain my child was in, I thought of how difficult it would have been for the Father to see His only Son bearing the pain of our sin on the cross.*

He knows! He understands! He chose to walk through these valleys before us. And when we walk into the darkest times of our lives, He never leaves us or forsakes us. He carries us (His lambs) in His arms, close to His heart.

A trial like this calls on parents to surrender what we are desperate to keep. Gradually, painfully, as we learn to worship the Giver more than His gift, we find His grace sufficient. But our hearts still ask, "Why my child?" It's good to ask why. God may give you the answer you crave—or as with Job, God may tell you to turn toward Him in the darkness and simply trust (Job 38-41).

Father Abraham did not ask any questions at all. Without question, argument, or delay, he got up early, gathered his supplies, and headed off with his son and servants on the three-day hike to Mt. Moriah (Gen. 22:3). Along the trail, did Abraham stare at his beloved son and question God? In Genesis 22:5, we get a hint of what Abraham was thinking. What in this verse suggests that he thought he would not be returning home alone?

What did Abraham believe God was going to do? (See Heb. 11:19.)

That's remarkable. We know about the resurrection of Jesus and of those He raised, but Abraham had never heard of anyone rising from the dead. How could he have conceived of such a thing?

First, Abraham's faith gave him "evidence of things not seen" (Heb. 11:1). Though he had never seen a resurrection, faith made it a reality to him. Also, Abraham knew that "in a figurative sense," like an object lesson, Isaac had been born to two "dead" parents (Heb. 11:19). Jehovah could once again give Isaac life from death.

Abraham and Isaac climbed the mountain prepared to make a sacrificial offering, the father carrying a knife and a burning torch, the son carrying dry wood on his back. When Isaac asked about the lamb they would need for the sacrifice, Abraham answered, "My son, God will provide for Himself the lamb for a burnt offering" (Gen. 22:8). That is faith. Undaunted, unflinching faith.

Abraham did not question the character of God because of his circumstances; he evaluated his circumstances in the light of Who he knew God to be. Unlike pagan gods, Jehovah did not demand human sacrifices. Unlike untrustworthy humans, God would never break His word. God could not be cruel, for He was good. God would never abandon or abuse His child, for He was love. How God would reconcile the command to kill Isaac with His own character was up to Him, but Abraham knew He would because he knew God.

On the mountaintop, Abraham bound Isaac, laid him on the wood of the altar they had built, "stretched out his hand and took the knife to slay his son" (Gen. 22:10). Isaac was submissive to his father, just as Abraham was submissive to God. Abraham was not pretending; he was fully expecting to kill his son.

We do not honor Abraham because he was willing to kill his son. We honor him for the faith it took to say "yes" when God asked him to do the unthinkable and for understanding that since God cannot break His covenants, Isaac would live. Somehow, Isaac would live.

And he did! God sent a ram headfirst into a thicket where it was caught by the horns. Abraham took hold of the ram and sacrificed it "for a burnt offering instead of his son" (Gen. 22:13). God had proved and honored Abraham's faith.

Abraham named that mountain site *Jehovah-Jireh*, which means *The Lord Will Provide*. Whatever you need—patience to wait for Him or courage to pass His tests—He will supply.

How is the scene on Mt. Moriah like the scene at Calvary?

> Surely He has borne our griefs and carried our sorrows; yet we esteemed Him stricken, smitten by God, and afflicted. But He was wounded for our transgressions, He was bruised for our iniquities; the chastisement for our peace was upon Him, and by His stripes we are healed. All we like sheep have gone astray; we have turned, every one, to his own way; and the Lord has laid on Him the iniquity of us all. (Isa. 53:4-6)

> Knowing that you were not redeemed with corruptible things, like silver or gold, from your aimless conduct received by tradition from your fathers, but with the precious blood of Christ, as of a lamb without blemish and without spot. (1 Pet. 1:18-19)

When this trial was over, God renewed His covenant with Abraham. For the fifth time, God pledged a land filled with multitudes of descendants who would bring blessings to all nations (Gen. 22:15-18). One of those blessings is Abraham's example of authentic faith.

When you are in pain, you might think God has forgotten you or does not love you. But the opposite is true—trials are a sure sign that He wants you to be His friend.

Think it through

What is the connection between faith, patience, and trials? (See Rom. 5:3-5 and James 1:2-4.)

CHAPTER EIGHT
The Vision of Faith: Isaac, Jacob, and Joseph

By faith he dwelt in the land of promise as in a foreign country,
dwelling in tents with Isaac and Jacob, the heirs with him of the same
promise; for he waited for the city which has foundations, whose
builder and maker is God. (Heb. 11:9-10)

These all died in faith, not having received the promises, but having seen
them afar off were assured of them, embraced them and confessed that
they were strangers and pilgrims on the earth. For those who say
such things declare plainly that they seek a homeland. And truly if
they had called to mind that country from which they had come out,
they would have had opportunity to return. But now they desire a better,
that is, a heavenly country. Therefore God is not ashamed to be called
their God, for He has prepared a city for them. (Heb. 11:13-16)

Abraham's family began to multiply just as God had promised. Abraham's
son Isaac fathered twin sons, Jacob and Esau. Jacob had many sons, including
Joseph who had sons of his own and whose position in Egypt made it possible
for Israel to grow into a nation of millions.

Abraham's descendants inherited the blessings of God's covenant, but they
could not inherit Abraham's friendship with God. Each person had to see
God individually, by faith. From the lives of Abraham's offspring we learn
this: *faith has vision.*

Like Abraham, you and I cannot pass along to our children and grandchildren
our relationship with God. But we can tell "the generation to come the praises
of the Lord, and His strength and His wonderful works that He has done . . .
that they may arise and declare them to their children, that they may set their
hope in God, and not forget the works of God, but keep His commandments"
(Psa. 78:4, 6-7). That is what God knew Abraham would do.

> For I have known him, in order that he may command his children and his household after him, that they keep the way of the Lord, to do righteousness and justice. (Gen. 18:19)

Imagine old Abraham sitting in his tent telling his family stories about the times he saw God! When you tell children stories about your life, always include the main character: God. Tell how you have seen God at work in your *past*. Teach them how to recognize Him when He shows up in their *now*. Encourage them to focus on Him more than on people, on eternity more than the present, and on their faith more than their doubts. Turn their vision from you to your God, and ask Him to reveal Himself to each of them.

Faith looks at what is ahead, not what is around

Abraham, Isaac, Jacob, and Joseph waited their whole lives for God to give them the land He had promised. Their faith survived the delay because it was focused on the future, not the present.

> How bold was their assurance! "Hello there, promise!" they cried. "We see you! You're ours! We welcome you!" The land was as safe and as sure as though they had already conquered and colonized it, because God had promised it. God's promissory notes are drawn by His own hand and cannot fail. A promise from God is a surer thing than a post-dated check from a billionaire.[1]

What was their lifestyle like? (See Heb. 11:9, 13.)

The Lord has called our family to an itinerant ministry. For years, our family home was an RV parked in church parking lots or anywhere we could find reasonably level ground. Now that the children have grown and gone, David and I travel in a car stuffed with suitcases stuffed with our stuff. I have learned two things from our peripatetic life: how to settle quickly into a short-term home and how to keep my roots from sinking in too deeply.

---

[1] Phillips, *Exploring Hebrews* (Moody, 1977), 170.

I don't stress over luxury or fret about perfection in temporary lodgings. Contentment comes easily when I remember that our own house is just a little farther down the highway. I will be there soon. That is how I want to live my life on earth—with contentment, remembering that every day brings me closer to my real home in heaven.

Christians are aliens on this planet.

> I am a stranger, with a stranger's indifference;
> My hands hold a pilgrim's staff,
> My march is Zionward,
> My eyes are toward the coming of the Lord.[2]

What is "a stranger's indifference"? What are a pilgrim's priorities?

These faith heroes could have gone back to their old home if they had wanted to, but they didn't. Why not? (See Heb. 11:15-16.)

The word *desire* in Hebrews 11:16 means *to stretch toward*, like a baby reaching for her mama. That is a sweet picture of a Christian longing for home.

Though the patriarchs looked forward to Canaan, their vision went beyond that small section of earth to the "city which has foundations, whose builder and maker is God" (Heb. 11:10). By faith, Christians are already citizens of a city Jesus has been preparing for more than two thousand years (Phil. 3:20, John 14:2-3).

---

[2] *The Valley of Vision,* ed. Arthur Bennett (Edinburgh: The Banner of Truth Trust, 1975), 198.

How did God feel about these men who lived for heaven rather than earth? (See Heb. 11:16.)

I give God plenty of reasons not to be proud of me, and the devil makes sure God knows them all. Accusing me is the devil's job (Rev. 12:10), but even he knows that my Savior has plans that include not only a brand-new home but also a brand-new me. Until then, I will not be perfect no matter how hard I try. But even an earthbound human like me can live down here with a vision of what is up there.

Faith looks at God, not self

We are about to visit men who were visited by God. Do not expect perfection from them; they had plenty of failures and crashes. Father Abraham did not rear perfect offspring. But despite their shortcomings, by the end of their lives they were focused on God, not themselves, and He was pleased to call Himself not only "the God of Abraham" but also "the God of Isaac, and the God of Jacob" (Exod. 3:6).

Isaac: an ordinary man with an extraordinary God

> By faith Isaac blessed Jacob and Esau concerning things to come. (Heb. 11:20)

Isaac was miraculously born to elderly parents and supernaturally rescued from dying as a burnt offering. His wife came to him in a remarkable way, and his sons were conceived through prayer. Those life events were extraordinary, but Isaac was an ordinary man.

Isaac had a passive, meditative disposition. He avoided confrontation and conflict, so he was easily manipulated and intimidated. Fear often caused him to do what was expedient rather than what was right. On his own, Isaac accomplished no great deeds of faith, but he was an heir of the covenant promises, and God met with him.

God's first appearance to Isaac is recorded in Genesis 26:1-5. What was the crisis? What was Isaac's plan to deal with it? (See Gen. 26:1.)

When God saw Isaac headed to a heathen king for help, He gave one command: stay in the land. Then He repeated the promises He had made to Abraham—His presence, the special land, and many descendants. Why was God going to do this for Isaac? (See Gen. 26:4-5.)

During another crisis, a serious quarrel over water rights, the Lord came again. How did He calm Isaac's fears? (See Gen. 26:24.)

Isaac's final vision came on his deathbed, which for many is a time of crisis and fear. This vision was of God's future blessings. His earlier visions had taught him to face life— and death—with faith in who God is and what He will do. Isaac's faith had grown.

When scary times come, fix your vision on God, not your problems, and your trials will nourish your faith. What makes you afraid today? Find a promise to claim. Read it over and over. Memorize it. Meditate on it. Peace will come.

> You will keep him in perfect peace, whose mind is stayed on You,
> because he trusts in You. Trust in the Lord forever, for in Jehovah,
> the Lord, is everlasting strength. (Isa. 26:3-4)

Jacob: an impatient man with a patient God

> By faith Jacob, when he was dying, blessed each of the sons of Joseph, and worshiped, leaning on the top of his staff. (Heb 11:21)

As he died, Jacob focused on God and others. That was a striking change for a man who spent most of his life consumed with himself. The flaw in Jacob's character was his determination to have things go his own way in his own time even if he had to manipulate others to get what he wanted.

Jacob was ambitious. After he emerged from his mother's womb holding on to his twin brother Esau's heel, trying to be born first, he was given a name meaning *supplanter*. From birth, Jacob was a usurper—one who schemes to oust someone else from his rightful place.

God had announced that in this family the older son would serve the younger, so Jacob knew early in life he was destined by God to inherit the wealth and family leadership that were privileges of the firstborn. Someday, Esau would be Jacob's servant. But Jacob, too impatient and weak in faith to wait for God to fulfill His prophecy, spent years trying to make it happen on his own.

To get what he wanted when he wanted it, Jacob lied, deceived, and took advantage of his brother's physical needs and his father's frailty (Gen. 25:29-34, Gen. 27:1-40). The results were awful. Esau became so murderously angry that Jacob had to run for his life. As he ran, God, Who also had reason to be furious with Jacob, appeared to him.

Read Genesis 28:10-22. What did Jacob see? (See Gen. 28:12.)

What did God call Himself? Why do you think He used that name? (See Gen. 28:13.)

God repeated the covenant promises to impatient, deceitful Jacob and added one more just for him: "I will not leave you until I have done what I have spoken to you" (Gen. 28:15). Jacob named that place Bethel (*house of God*). What vows did he make there? (See Gen. 28:20-22.)

God also appeared to Jacob during other crises. When after many years the Angel of God (the pre-incarnate Jesus) told Jacob to bring his family back to the land of promise, He called Himself "the God of Bethel" (Gen. 31:13). Why do you think He used that name?

On the way back, afraid at the prospect of seeing his brother Esau again, Jacob stopped twice. The first time, he paused to pray. Read his prayer in Genesis 32:9-12. How had this man changed? Now where was his focus?

Jacob sent his family ahead then stopped again at the edge of a brook, where he had an all-night physical wrestling match with a spiritual being. Read Genesis 32:24-32. By daybreak, the contest was over, and Jacob was different. He had a new limp, a new name, and a transformed character. His battle with self was done. Now all he wanted was God's blessing.

Jacob came back to Bethel, just as God had said he would. Read Genesis 35:9-15. Jacob now knew that all his plotting and conniving had been unnecessary. God was perfectly able to keep His promises without Jacob's help. All Jacob needed was faith in Him. On his deathbed, Jacob blessed his descendants, then died, an impatient man who finally understood that God was worthy of trust.

God will do what He will do, and He will do it in His time. Are you waiting for God to do something? Impatiently, maybe? Have you been so preoccupied with what you long for that you have schemed and manipulated to get it? Do not repeat Jacob's mistakes. Relax, have faith, and watch God go to work for you.

<u>*Joseph: a wronged man with a righteous God*</u>

> By faith Joseph, when he was dying, made mention of the departure of the children of Israel, and gave instructions concerning his bones. (Heb. 11:22)

Joseph was Jacob's eleventh and favorite son. By the time he was seventeen, his brothers were so jealous of Joseph they could hardly speak to him. It didn't help when he tattled on them, and things only got worse after Joseph told them about two of his dreams. Read Genesis 37:5-11. These were not fantasies but prophecies—visions of what God was going to do. Joseph had faith that they would come true.

But the next thirteen years of Joseph's life were wretched. His brothers sold him into slavery and told their father that his favorite son had been eaten by a wild animal. In Egypt, Joseph was falsely accused of rape, imprisoned, and forgotten. Any one of those trials would have been enough to send me over the edge. How do you think Joseph survived?

In the providence of God, Joseph was finally freed and given an exalted position in Egypt. His trials did not make him into a man of faith; they revealed spiritual strength that had always been there.

A pastor friend wrote this during chemotherapy treatments.

> *I often thought that if I contracted a disease like cancer that the disease would either immobilize me with fear or turn me into a spiritual giant like I've read about in missionary biographies. But I've found that in the long run not much changes. We are who we are. The only thing that changes who we are is spiritual discipline, not adverse or joy-filled*

circumstances. However, the circumstances do a pretty good job at revealing who we are!

Joseph's brothers did not recognize him when they came to Egypt seeking food, but he knew them. When they "bowed down before him with their faces to the earth" (Gen. 42:6), the vision that had sustained Joseph for so long became reality. His faith was made sight.

As he lay dying, Joseph shared another faith vision with his brothers. The God Who had kept His promises to Joseph had plans for them, too.

> And Joseph said to his brethren, "I am dying; but God will surely visit you, and bring you out of this land to the land of which He swore to Abraham, to Isaac, and to Jacob." (Gen. 50:24)

And Joseph went with them. His bones were carted around the wilderness by the children of Israel. His coffin waited on the edge of battlefields as they fought God's enemies. Long after his death, this man of enduring faith finally entered the Promised Land.

> The bones of Joseph, which the children of Israel had brought up out of Egypt, they buried at Shechem, in the plot of ground . . . which had become an inheritance of the children of Joseph. (Josh. 24:32)

Joseph's life was a complicated, bewildering journey, but God sustained him.

Although Abraham, Isaac, Jacob, and Joseph lived long ago in a world vastly different from ours, our stresses and trials are not that different from theirs. Remember this when you are going through a hard time: the God of these ancient men is your God, too. Keep your eyes fixed on Him.

Think it through

What makes it hard for you to stay focused on eternity rather than earth? On God rather than on people?

CHAPTER NINE
The Courage of Faith: Moses

> By faith Moses, when he was born, was hidden three months by his parents, because they saw he was a beautiful child; and they were not afraid of the king's command. By faith Moses, when he became of age, refused to be called the son of Pharaoh's daughter, choosing rather to suffer affliction with the people of God than to enjoy the passing pleasures of sin, esteeming the reproach of Christ greater riches than the treasures in Egypt; for he looked to the reward. By faith he forsook Egypt, not fearing the wrath of the king; for he endured as seeing Him who is invisible. By faith he kept the Passover and the sprinkling of blood, lest he who destroyed the firstborn should touch them. By faith they passed through the Red Sea as by dry land, whereas the Egyptians, attempting to do so, were drowned. (Heb. 11:23-29)

Many Hebrews 11 faith heroes were brave, but Moses is probably the best model of our next principle of faith: *faith has courage.*

While he was a ruler in Egypt, Joseph had brought his father Jacob and his brothers with their families to live near him. They grew from an extended family of seventy people into a nation of about two million living within the borders of another nation. They "were fruitful and increased abundantly, multiplied and grew exceedingly mighty; and the land was filled with them" (Exod. 1:7).

By that time, "Joseph died, all his brothers, and all that generation" (Exod. 1:6). The new Pharaoh felt no obligation to Joseph's descendants. What he saw through his palace windows was a horde of foreigners living the good life in his land.

To eliminate this threat to his kingdom, Pharaoh made the Israelites slaves—forced laborers whose lives became "bitter with hard bondage" (Exod. 1:13-

14). Did his plan to destroy Israel work? How did God take care of His people? (See Exod. 1:12.)

So Pharaoh devised a more ruthless strategy. Read Exodus 1:15-21. How did God protect His children?

Then came another unthinkably horrible decree—every newborn Jewish male was to be thrown into the Nile, to drown or be eaten by crocodiles. Parents were shocked and terrified. Where was Jehovah? How would He protect their babies? For many, I am sure, faith was buried under panic and despair. But one Hebrew couple was different. Their faith showed itself in remarkable, creative courage.

Faith has courage to risk

This couple was Amram and Jochebed, Moses' parents and his models of faith.

> By faith Moses, when he was born, was hidden three months by his parents, because they saw he was a beautiful child; and they were not afraid of the king's command. (Heb. 11:23)

Determined to protect their "beautiful child" (Exod. 2:2), Amram and Jochebed refused to let him be killed. They knew Pharaoh as a brutal monarch who would not hesitate to kill them and their baby, but they feared God more than they feared the kill order of a tyrant.

They hid their son at home for three months, then when he was too big (and loud) to be hidden anymore, devised a plan to save his life. Mother Jochebed swaddled her baby, tucked him into a basket of bulrushes waterproofed with pitch, and set the basket afloat near Pharaoh's daughter's bathing spot. Big sister Miriam stood nearby watching her baby brother's basket bobbing among the river reeds. This was dangerous. There were crocodiles. The baby could wiggle and overturn his floating cradle. Maybe the princess would be cruel.

The plan was risky. It might not work. But Moses' parents confronted risk and doubt with confidence in the Almighty, and that is what faith is all about.

> There is no need for faith where there is no consciousness of an element of risk. Faith, to be worthy of the name, must embrace doubt.[1]

When the baby cried, his cry touched the heart of the princess. She claimed him as her own and gave him the name that has been famous ever since— Moses. That day at the river, God set in motion His plan to deliver His people. He saved one tiny boy who, right under Pharaoh's nose, grew up to be the liberator of Pharaoh's slaves. Pharaoh had unlimited power in Egypt, but God's providence governs the world. From helpless babies to mighty monarchs, He rules over all.

> You, whose name alone is the Lord, are the Most High over all the earth. (Psa. 83:18)

God gave Moses parents with faith. Though they could not see God's big plan, faith assured them He had one, and that gave them courage to do right even when it was risky. When the time comes for you to take a bold step, and you're scared to take it, remember Amram and Jochebed. Find out what God wants you to do, then just do it.

Faith has courage to refuse

Jochebed's faith was rewarded. The princess accepted Miriam's offer to find a nurse for Moses, and Jochebed was paid to mother her own baby in her own home. Moses lived with his birth family until he "grew, and she [Jochebed] brought him to Pharaoh's daughter, and he became her son" (Exod. 2:10).

---

[1] Elisabeth Elliot, *The Savage My Kinsman* (Ann Arbor, MI: Servant Publications, 1961), 63.

That was a hard day. This goodbye took an extra measure of faith, for Moses' parents were releasing their son to be adopted by idol-worshipers, knowing that in Pharaoh's palace Moses would be surrounded by the enticements of lust, wealth, and power. How do you think Jochebed, knowing that this day would come, prepared Moses? What would she have taught her little boy while he was still with her?

We do not know how old Moses was when he moved to the palace, but he was old enough to understand that he was different from the Egyptians. Though the temptations of life at court were intense, this young prince saw them through the lens of truth learned from his mother. "By faith" what did he refuse and reject? What did he choose and value instead? What did he look forward to? (See Heb. 11:25-26.)

Faith has courage to act

Educated in the court of Pharaoh, Moses became "learned in all the wisdom of the Egyptians and was mighty in words and deeds" (Acts 7:22) but still maintained a heart connection with his enslaved relatives. Along with every other Israelite child, Moses had been taught this prophecy and promise of God:

> Then He said to Abram: "Know certainly that your descendants will be strangers in a land that is not theirs, and will serve them, and they will afflict them four hundred years. And also the nation whom they serve I will judge; afterward they shall come out with great possessions." (Gen. 15:13-14)

The Israelites knew they would not be slaves forever. Someday they would escape, taking Egyptian treasure with them. Moses believed he was destined to lead this flight to freedom, that the people would acknowledge him as their God-sent leader and follow him out of Egypt.

When Moses was forty years old, something happened that exposed flaws in his character. Read the original story in Exodus 2:11-15 and Stephen's retelling of it in Acts 7:23-29.

How did Moses feel toward the Israelite slaves? (See Acts 7:23 and Exod. 2:11.)

What motivated his attack on the Egyptian? (See Acts 7:24.)

How did he expect the Israelites to respond? (See Acts 7:25.)

That day in the desert, Moses acted impulsively, in fleshly fury and ambition rather than in faith. Faith-based courage acts only in God's will. Even if it's done with good motives, sin is still sin. Murder is still murder. Moses tried to cover his crime (literally) by burying the dead Egyptian in the sand, but God saw what he did. So did one of the Hebrews, and the next day, Moses was exposed as a killer. Rather than welcoming him as their deliverer, the Israelites resented his trying to become "a ruler and a judge" over them (Acts 7:27).

Condemned to death by Pharaoh, Moses bolted. He wound up in Midian, where he spent the next forty years herding sheep in the desert. By trying to get God's work done in his own strength rather than through faith, by acting prematurely rather than patiently, Moses had made a mess.

Faith has courage to lead

In Midian, God humbled Moses and transformed his carnal brashness into the bold but patient courage of genuine faith. Read Exodus 2:23-3:17.

In an isolated, barren part of Midian, Moses saw an extraordinary sight: a desert bush burning but not consumed. He heard a voice calling his name, answered, "Here I am," and hid his face. The Angel of the Lord spoke from the bush. "I have seen My people's suffering," He said. "I have heard their cries. I'm going to deliver them and take them home." This was good news. But what came next was startling. What was Moses' assignment from God? (See Exod. 3:10.)

The old Moses would have jumped at the chance, but the new Moses didn't. List his objections and God's answers to them.

Exodus 3:11-12—

Exodus 3:13-14—

Exodus 4:1-9—

Exodus 4:10-16—

God responded to each of Moses' protests by pointing him to Himself: "I will certainly be with you" (Exod. 3:12). The great *I AM,* the self-existent, eternal God wanted Moses to have faith in Him, not in himself.

Moses went back to Egypt knowing God was ready to work. When he demonstrated the miraculous signs God had given him, "the people believed; and when they heard that the Lord had visited the children of Israel and that He had looked on their affliction, then they bowed their heads and worshiped" (Exod. 4:31). It was time. Now they were ready to follow Moses. Moses had always had faith he would be their leader. He had just been wrong about the timing.

Immediately, confrontations with Pharaoh began. Again and again, Moses demanded the slaves' release; over and over, Pharaoh refused and made their lives even harder. Angry and disappointed, the Israelites turned on Moses. His faith was shaken, and he interrogated God. *Where are You? What's going on? You promised, but I can't see You doing anything!*

Read Exodus 6:1-8. How did God respond to Moses' frustration?

When the plagues began, Pharaoh discovered he was battling a power superior to his own. Water turned to blood. Frogs, lice, and flies smothered the land. Livestock died. Boils covered men and beasts. Hail destroyed crops and locusts consumed the harvest. Days of darkness brought terror. But still Pharaoh refused to let the people go.

Moses forecast the plagues one at a time. He would say, "Thus says the Lord," then announce what was coming next. Think of the courage it took to announce publicly what God was going to do before it happened. What a risk! But God did what He had said, and with each fulfillment of prophecy, Moses' faith grew stronger. But the hardest test was to come. What final prediction did Moses make? (See Exod. 11:4-8.)

All the other plagues were tolerable compared to this one, and there was only one way to escape its horror. Read Exodus 12:21-23. This was a serious test of Moses' leadership. If Moses did not hear and deliver God's words correctly and persuade the Israelites to obey them, many would die. Only faith could give Moses the courage he needed.

> By faith he kept the Passover and the sprinkling of blood, lest he
> who destroyed the firstborn should touch them. (Heb. 11:28)

When death wails began to rise all over the land, Pharaoh gave in, and exactly at the prophesied time, Israel left captivity (Exod. 12:40-41). They left their chains behind, but in fulfillment of prophecy, what did they take with them? (See Exod. 12:35-36.)

Moses led the throng of freed slaves as they followed God's cloud by day and His fire by night. They were headed to the Promised Land. At the edge of the Red Sea, they halted, stunned. Water—too wide to go around and too deep to wade through. From behind "the Egyptians pursued them, all the horses and chariots of Pharaoh, his horsemen and his army" (Exod. 14:9). Pharaoh had changed his mind. The Israelites were trapped.

Read Exodus 14:10-14. What was the attitude of the people as they stood on the edge of the impossible?

Moses spoke with confidence to the panicked, complaining congregation. Read Exodus 14:13-14. Where did he turn the people's attention? What did he have faith God would do?

What kind of man was Moses when he was forty? (See Acts 7:25.)

When he was eighty? (See Exod. 3:11.)

What is he like now, at the edge of the Red Sea?

Moses is still bold, but his confidence is no longer in himself. Now his faith is only in God. "Moses spent forty years in the king's palace thinking that he was somebody; then he lived forty years in the wilderness finding out that without God he was a nobody; finally he spent forty more years discovering how a nobody with God can be a somebody."[2]

The more faith you have in God, the less you will have in yourself. It takes time to learn this. During his son's difficult cancer treatments, a pastor learned this lesson.

> *I have studied and taught the Bible for the last forty years. One of the best things about getting older or going through a difficult time is seeing scriptural truths in a more colorful, textured context. During these months, many simple, familiar passages have taken on a slightly more personal nuance.*
>
> *Yesterday I was thinking of the familiar opening words of James 1:2–4. It occurred to me (not for the first time but in a deeper way) that there is only one test going on here. This is not a test of my strength, leadership, wisdom, endurance, toughness, influence, financial wherewithal, or intellect—it is a test of my FAITH. It is not a test of what I am capable of but whether or not I am willing to place my trust (faith) in the only One who is worthy of the responsibility and weight of caring for the dear child that He gave us. Better Him than me!*

---

[2] "Dwight L. Moody." AZQuotes.com. Wind and Fly LTS, 2020. 01 October 2020. https://www.azquotes.com/author/10304-Dwight_L_Moody

That is the essence of faith. We often think of people strong in faith as if they have MORE of something that others don't have, but the reality is they have less! There is less strength and more weakness. (His strength is made perfect in weakness. His grace is sufficient.) Ironically, what they have more of is less of self.

Moses' faith was strong toward God because it was weak toward himself. His faith spread across the nation.

> Thus Israel saw the great work which the Lord had done in Egypt; so the people feared the Lord, and believed the Lord and His servant Moses. (Exod. 14:31)

Few of us are naturally bold. We're mostly a timid bunch. Knowing that we are not competent in ourselves, we fear failure. But sometimes, somebody has to have enough faith to *do* something. Moses faced a time like that. Someday, you will too.

Think it through

Someday (maybe today), you are going to be given a job that requires more courage than you have. When that day comes, what will you do?

CHAPTER TEN
Joshua and Rahab

The Battles of Faith: Joshua

By faith the walls of Jericho fell down after they were encircled for seven days.
(Heb. 11:30)

Faith gives courage to fight enemies within and without. *Faith battles.* Christians are not alone on their battlefield. The God with unlimited power and a perfect strategy fights for us. Through faith in Him, we can have victory. That is what we learn from our next faith hero, Joshua, and the battle of Jericho.

As we ended our last chapter, the nation of Israel had just been supernaturally delivered from slavery in Egypt. After reaching the other shore of the Red Sea, they celebrated with victory songs, then began the trek toward their new home. If they had known that forty years later they would still be scrambling over barren hills and trudging through desert sands, they might not have had the courage to take the first step.

But all the way, all those years in the wilderness, God watched over His people. Food fell from the sky, water gushed from rocks, clothes didn't fall apart, and sandals didn't disintegrate. Sometimes they praised the divine Provider; other times they griped about what He gave.

Through all their struggles, victories, and defeats, they had one constant: Moses. Organizer, overseer, builder, and intercessor, Moses led as the people moved vaguely toward the land of promise. But Moses never took a step into Canaan. After an episode of angry disobedience near the end of the journey, Moses learned that God would not allow him to enter the land (Num. 20:7-

12). After one long look at Canaan, Moses died, and Israel turned to their new leader: Joshua.

Joshua had a history with the people. Much earlier, when "Amalek came and fought with Israel in Rephidim" (Exod. 17:8), Joshua had led the Israeli army. While Moses stood at the top of a hill holding up the rod of God, "Joshua defeated Amalek and his people with the edge of the sword" (Exod. 17:13).

Joshua was one of the twelve men Moses had sent to scout out the land. All of them saw fortressed cities defended by fierce, giant warriors. They also saw amazing fruit growing in the land—pomegranates, figs, and clusters of grapes so large they had to be carried on a pole (Num. 13:23).

Two of the spies, Joshua and Caleb, came back fueled by the excitement of faith. "Sure, there are enemies out there, and they are huge! But Canaan flows with milk and honey and grows fruit like you would not believe. Besides, the God of the Red Sea has already guaranteed us the victory, so we can't lose. Let's go! Let's do it!" They begged the people to move forward in faith.

But the other ten spies predicted gloom and doom, disaster and defeat. They saw the giants in the land as bigger than their God. "We're like grasshoppers compared to them," they said. "They'll eat us up!" (Num. 13:32-33). The people listened to the ten rather than the two, whined, wailed, and refused to budge. They even threatened to stone Joshua and Caleb. What price did those faithless folks pay? (See Num. 14:26-38.)

For forty years (a year for each day the spies spied), Israel wandered a barren land. Parents who had moaned that their children would die in the wilderness died themselves instead and were left behind in hundreds of thousands of graves strewn across the desert. Only two adults alive at the Red Sea crossing also crossed the Jordan into Canaan: Caleb and our hero Joshua.

Faith's battles are first fought in private

Joshua's first battles were with his own doubts and fears. When he saw the giant enemies occupying Canaan, his faith in Jehovah proved stronger than his fear of defeat. When the people mocked and wanted to kill him for urging them to enter the land, he did not surrender to the pressure of the crowd.

Joshua defeated the temptation to retreat when God said to move forward. He resisted the impulse to abandon his convictions and blend in with an unbelieving crowd. The secret to his later public victories as general over Israel's army—including the battle of Jericho—was that he first won his private battles with unbelief.

Soon after Moses' death, the Lord spoke to Joshua, giving him his commission and the keys to success in leading Israel. What command did God give Joshua three times? (See Josh. 1:6, 7, 9.)

That is a big order, one that is impossible for any human, no matter how gifted in leadership, to do alone, so God also gave Joshua a promise—twice. What was it? (See Josh. 1:5, 9.)

What daily habit would bring Joshua prosperity and success? (See Josh. 1:8.)

Joshua had only the Law of Moses, but your Bible has sixty-six books! What are you supposed to do with them? If you do, what good things will happen?

> Blessed is the man who walks not in the counsel of the ungodly,
> nor stands in the path of sinners, nor sits in the seat of the scorn-
> ful; but his delight is in the law of the Lord, and in His law he

meditates day and night. He shall be like a tree planted by the rivers of water, that brings forth its fruit in its season, whose leaf also shall not wither; and whatever he does shall prosper. (Psa. 1:1-3)

If you are consistently losing personal battles over the enemies of your faith, the key to victory may be as simple as spending more time with your nose in the Book. Joshua meditated on God's Word and delighted in God in private, and victories of faith followed.

Faith's battles demand personal holiness

Three days after God's conversation with Joshua, the people lined up to cross the Jordan into Canaan. Leading the way were priests carrying the symbol of God's presence—the ark of the covenant. As soon as they had taken their first soggy steps, the river stopped flowing and stood at attention as the whole nation "hurried and crossed over" (Josh. 4:10). The journey from Egypt to Canaan ended just as it started, with a display of God's power.

Following God's directions, Joshua set up a twelve-stone memorial so the twelve tribes would never forget this miracle of deliverance. Energized by what they had just seen and eager to get going, forty thousand armed men were preparing for battle when Joshua abruptly halted the march into Canaan and ordered camp to be set up at Gilgal.

What did the people need to do before battling? (See Josh. 5:2-9.)

Why did this matter? (See Gen. 17:9-14.)

Circumcision was the physical symbol God had chosen to set His people apart from the heathen around them. In the same way, the holiness of our hearts, revealed by our obedient lives, sets us apart from the world around us.

God told Israel:
You shall be holy, for I the Lord your God am holy. (Lev. 19:2)

God tells us:
But as He who called you is holy, you also be holy in all your conduct, because it is written, "Be holy, for I am holy." (1 Pet. 1:15-16)

What did Israel do next? (See Josh. 5:10.)

Even before the first Passover night, God had told Israel to re-enact it every year, forever (Exod. 12:14, 17, 42). Keeping the Passover was more than a ritual. It was both a reminder to fear the God Who had delivered them from bondage and an act of obedience. During the wilderness years, the Israelites had not observed the Passover.

What happened the day after they kept the first Passover in their own land? (See Josh. 5:11-12.)

For forty years, the people had not had to provide their own food. Every day without fail, manna had appeared on the ground. From now on, though, they would have to provide for themselves. A new life was beginning, one that would call for a new level of faith.

The Israelites' camp was only a few miles from Jericho, the huge Canaanite city that blocked Israel's passage into the land. The Israelites were not well-armed, seasoned warriors, but only a band of weary wanderers who had just stumbled out of the desert. Conquering Jericho seemed impossible, even to these folks who had just seen at the Jordan what their God could do. But Joshua was an experienced general who had proved himself capable in battle, so just as they had trusted Moses, they trusted Joshua to come up with a plan.

> Now Joshua the son of Nun was full of the spirit of wisdom, for Moses had laid his hands on him; so the children of Israel heeded him. (Deut. 34:9)

Faith's battles are fought God's way

As much fortress as city, Jericho was surrounded by massive stone bulwarks. No battering ram could breach Jericho's double and triple gates. To attack the city, an army would have to catapult boulders over its thick walls or burrow under them. Soldiers trying to climb the walls risked being pierced by arrows or scalded by hot oil.

General Joshua had already sent two spies into Jericho on a reconnaissance mission, and they had returned with a surprising report. How were "all the inhabitants of the land" reacting to this crowd of people camping in their territory? Why? (See Josh. 2:24, 5:1, 6:1.)

Planning his strategy, Joshua moved closer to see the enemy city for himself. An unfamiliar soldier suddenly appeared carrying a sword. "Whose side are you on?" Joshua demanded. Who did the soldier say He was? How did Joshua respond? (See Josh. 5:13-15.)

Jesus, the Commander of angel armies, had come in pre-incarnate form to guarantee victory if Joshua did what he was told. This was going to be a battle of faith rather than a military campaign. The tactics laid out in Joshua 6:3-5 were extraordinary. If they had not come from God Himself, they would have been ridiculous.

Each day for seven days, seven priests blowing seven rams' horns marched once around the city walls carrying the ark of the covenant. Armed men guarded the front and rear, but no one spoke or used a weapon. At dawn on the seventh day, this strange parade circled the locked-down, bewildered city seven times. At the last step, the priests blasted their horns and the soldiers let loose a shout of triumph.

And Jericho's walls fell flat! Gigantic stone fortifications rumbled to the ground. Open and vulnerable, the city was quickly spoiled, not by an army but by faith. No words are truer than these from Joshua, "The Lord has given you the city!" (Josh. 6:16). Nothing but the hand of God could have knocked down those walls. What happened was humanly impossible. The strategy was strange, but God's way of victory worked—as it always does.

> For the weapons of our warfare are not carnal [human] but mighty in God for pulling down strongholds. (2 Cor. 10:4)

> Not by might nor by power, but by My Spirit, says the Lord of hosts. (Zech. 4:6)

The Life-Changing Power of Faith: Rahab

> By faith the harlot Rahab did not perish with those who did not believe, when she had received the spies with peace. (Heb. 11:31)

Every battle you win by faith has an impact on others. Believers watching you will be encouraged to fight their own battles God's way, and God will use the testimony of your victory to draw people to Himself, sometimes in a remarkable way, for *faith changes lives.*

Rahab was an unlikely convert, but she was a seeking soul, and God had a plan for her.

An unlikely convert

Read the first part of Rahab's story in Joshua 2:1-23. This passage raises some issues. The first is that the Israelite spies spent the night in the house of a harlot. Even back then, even among pagans, prostitution was shameful. The Bible does not condone Rahab's lifestyle; it just tells us frankly who she was.

The spies knew God's command against immorality, so why would they stay in Rahab's house? Jericho was on guard against invasion, so its citizens were watching for infiltrators. Since her house was often visited by strangers, it was a place the spies could be anonymous while gathering information. Rahab's house was on the city wall, which offered a quick escape route if they needed it. And we cannot overlook the most obvious explanation: God saw faith growing in Rahab's heart and sent the men to help her.

Another question we have is about Rahab's lie (Josh. 2:4-6). Once again God's Word simply tells us what happened, without explanation or excuse. Rahab was living a sinful life in a pagan city, and she lied. But God used her to protect His servants.

A seeking soul

What had Rahab heard about Israel and their God? (See Josh. 2:8-10.)

What did Rahab ask the spies to do? (Josh. 2:12-13.)

Rahab had intelligence and spiritual insight. She was not the only one who had trembled at the news of what Israel's God could do, but she—maybe only she—believed He was the true sovereign God. "For the Lord *[Jehovah]* your God *[Elohim]*, He is God in heaven above and on earth beneath" (Josh. 2:11).

That is a remarkable statement of faith from a Gentile harlot. Rahab knew nothing else about the God of Israel. She just knew she and her family were doomed unless He saved them, and the only way she knew to reach Him was through the two men who had come to her house. Rahab hid the spies, agreed to their rescue plan, and sent them safely on their way. Then her faith took its first step of obedience. As the men had instructed, she hung a scarlet cord from a window of her house (Josh 2:21).

Read the second part of Rahab's story in Joshua 6:16-25. The crimson rope in her window was a symbol of the faith that saved Rahab and her family from death, just as the crimson blood of a lamb on the doorposts of Hebrew homes was the symbol of the faith that delivered their sons from death (Exod. 12:23). Today, anyone who by faith applies the crimson blood of the perfect Lamb of God to her sinful heart will be saved from eternal death (1 John 1:7).

Rahab knew little about Jehovah God. How big does faith have to be for God to honor it? (See Matt. 17:20.)

Who does God specialize in saving? (See Matt. 9:10-13.)

A part of God's plan

Rahab, the first recorded Gentile convert, became part of the Jewish community (Josh. 6:25). She is even listed in the "begots" of Matthew 1:1-6.

Rahab married _____. Their son was _____, who married _____.

Their son was _____. His son was _____, and his son was _____.

A converted Gentile harlot became the great-great-grandmother of the greatest king of Israel! Another of Rahab's descendants was Joseph, the legal (not natural) father of Jesus (Matt. 1:16). Jehovah saw a tiny seed of faith in Rahab, saved her, transformed her family tree, and offers her to us as a heroine.

Think it through

Are you in a faith battle right now? What can you do to increase your chance of having victory? Who will be affected by your victory or failure?

Have you ever thought that sin in your past prohibits you from serving God today? How can the story of fallible but faithful Rahab help you?

Facing Your Enemies

You are in a perpetual battle with three enemies that are trying to keep you from entering Canaan, your own promised land. Canaan is not a symbol of heaven—no child of God has to fight her way into her eternal home—but of the sweet, blessed place of victory in the Christian life.

Your enemies do not carry spears and swords, but they are powerful and closer than you think. They are giants, but they are not invincible. You can defeat them if you will follow God's battle strategies.

The world

This is not the natural world, but the *kosmos*—this world's culture with its unholy attitudes and pleasures, its unrighteous values and viewpoints.

Why does this enemy hate you? (See John 15:18-21.)

What are the Bible strategies for victory over the world?

2 Timothy 3:12-17–

1 John 2:15-17—

1 John 5:4-5—

The flesh

This is not skin and bones, but the *sarx*, any part of you that is not spirit. Your flesh and your spirit are in constant conflict.

> For the flesh lusts against the Spirit, and the Spirit against the flesh; and these are contrary to one another. (Gal. 5:17)

Read Romans 7:14-25. Does Paul's struggle sound familiar? Your flesh tugs at you to do wrong while your spirit wants you to do right. Read Galatians 5:19-23, and you will see that your flesh is capable of rottenness, but through the Holy Spirit, you can bear sweet fruit instead.

What are the Bible strategies for victory over your flesh?

Romans 8:13—

Romans 13:14—

Galatians 5:16—

The devil

He is *Satan, Beelzebub, Lucifer, accuser, adversary, serpent, tempter, ruler of this world, father of lies, the wicked one*—the devil has many names and wears many disguises.

What is he doing right now? (See 1 Pet. 5:8.)

What are the Bible strategies for victory over the devil?

Ephesians 6:11-18—

1 Peter 5:8-9—

James 4:7—

Yet in all these things we are more than conquerors through Him who loved us. (Rom. 8:37)

CHAPTER ELEVEN
The Victories of Faith

And what more shall I say? For the time would fail me to tell of Gideon and
Barak and Samson and Jephthah, also of David and Samuel and the prophets:
who through faith subdued kingdoms, worked righteousness, obtained promises,
stopped the mouths of lions, quenched the violence of fire, escaped the edge of the
sword, out of weakness were made strong, became valiant in battle, turned to flight
the armies of the aliens. Women received their dead raised to life again.
(Heb. 11:32-35a)

We are coming to the end of our tour of faith's hall of fame and need to hurry
along, for there are still many heroes to meet and much to learn from them.
In our concluding chapters, we will zoom over centuries of Bible history.

Hebrews 11:32-35a introduces us to heroes whose lives and exploits illustrate
this: *faith wins.* We'll focus on their victories now. In the middle of verse 35,
the writer shifts to those who were defeated, or *seemed* to be. We'll look at
their sufferings and losses next time.

Remember this: each person in Hebrews 11, whether triumphant or
vanquished, was a true hero. Faith does not guarantee outward success. God's
perspective is different from ours, and sometimes in His providence, He
allows the faithful to fail—or *seem* to fail.

Also remember this: some who won public victories over God's enemies lost
private battles with besetting sins. God still honors them, for He looks for
faith, not perfection. That's encouraging!

Before he died, Joshua had promised Israel that if they would be brave, obey
the Law, and "hold fast to the Lord," God would fight for them (Josh. 23:8).

They promised they would, but over and over, they failed. Whenever they repented and cried for help, God "raised up judges who delivered them out of the hand of those who plundered them" (Judg. 2:16). The judges were followed by prophets and kings. God never abandoned His people or left them without a leader even when they disappointed Him. Six of the men God sent to help Israel are named in Hebrews 11:32.

Gideon

When Gideon appeared on the scene, Israel had suffered through seven miserable years. Midianites "as numerous as locusts" (Judg. 6:5) had regularly wiped out Israel's crops and livestock. Forced to live in "the dens, the caves, and the strongholds which are in the mountains" (Judg. 6:2), Israel cried for a deliverer. God sent Gideon.

The Angel of the Lord (later identified as God Himself) found Gideon hiding under a tree threshing a little pile of wheat. The Angel called Gideon a "mighty man of valor" (Judg. 6:12) though he looked hungry and desperate instead. He told Gideon, "The Lord is with you!" but Gideon doubted that. What were his complaints? (See Judg. 6:13.)

Ignoring Gideon's misgivings, the Angel gave him a commission: "Go in this might of yours, and you shall save Israel from the hand of the Midianites. Have I not sent you?" (Judg. 6:14). Gideon did not want to go. What excuse did he make? (See Judg. 6:15.)

The Angel offered two guarantees: "Surely I will be with you, and you shall defeat the Midianites" (Judg. 6:16). What did Gideon ask for? (See Judg. 6:17.)

So far Gideon seems to be a man with no faith at all.

> He doubted God's presence. *If the Lord is with us, then why . . . ?*
> He doubted God's character. *If God is so powerful, then why. . . ?*
> He doubted God's enabling. *I can't. I'm the youngest one in the poorest family around here.*
> He doubted God's call. *I need proof. Show me your ID.*

After a supernatural sign of fire (Judg. 6:20-21), Gideon finally believed his visitor was divine, but he still was not convinced of God's power. After gathering his army, Gideon asked for still one more sign. God gave him two: the fleece (Judg. 6:36-40) and the dream (Judg. 7:9-15).

It is easy to see why Gideon needed reassurance. The well-armed Midianite army was 135,000 strong, but Gideon had three hundred men with trumpets, pitchers, and torches. If God did not come through for them, Israel did not stand a chance. Finally, Gideon rose above his doubts and fears to rouse his army. "Arise, for the Lord has delivered the camp of Midian into your hand" (Judg. 7:15). Notice that Gideon used the past tense *before* the battle. What kind of faith did Gideon have now? (See Heb. 11:1.)

Gideon had doubts, but God saw his faith and used him. Do you have doubts? God can use you!

Barak

Judge Barak is usually linked with Deborah, a judge and prophetess. Their story is in Judges 4.

This time Israel's enemies were the idol-worshiping Canaanites. Their army had nine hundred chariots—ironclad war machines pulled by ten horses, manned by expert archers, and fitted with razor-sharp blades spinning from each wheel. For twenty years this army commanded by Sisera had "harshly oppressed the children of Israel" (Judg. 4:3). This enemy was powerful but doomed.

> Woe to those who . . . rely on horses, who trust in chariots because they are many, and in horsemen because they are very strong, but who do not look to the Holy One of Israel, nor seek the Lord! (Isa. 31:1)

Deborah gave Barak two messages from God: a command to take ten thousand troops and fight Sisera "with his chariots and his multitude" (Judg. 4:6-7) and a promise to "deliver him into your hand" (Judg. 4:7). Barak responded to Deborah, "If you will not go with me, I will not go!" (Judg. 4:8). That wasn't as cowardly as it sounds. Barak faced impossible odds and needed Deborah to come along to boost his faith.

God gave victory. By the end of the conflict, the enemy army was dead, except for Sisera, who ran until he was exhausted and then collapsed in an ally's tent. If you are up to it, read the gory story of Jael, a woman who used her wiles and her strong arms to kill Sisera (Judg. 4:17-22). Using one judge, ten thousand soldiers, and two women with faith, God "routed Sisera and all his chariots and all his army with the edge of the sword" (Judg. 4:15).

Everyone's faith gets wobbly now and then. Even faith heroes like Barak sometimes shake in their shoes. But we can obey our Commander even when we are afraid.

A pastor's wife in the Midwest tells this story.

> *Our friend turned ninety-six years old today. He is not related to us, but he might as well be. He is part of our sweet church family, which is basically the same thing: family.*

> *We took him out to eat—to his favorite restaurant—to eat his preferred hot beef sandwich. As we were walking out, a man saw our friend's hat and thanked him for his military service.*

Our friend shared with the man that he had served in World War II and fought in the Battle of the Bulge. (He also was there when they liberated concentration camps. He saw firsthand what was left of a person who endured such a camp. His description is too much to share.)

He is quite an extraordinary man who deserves to be honored, but he responded, "We were only twenty and scared."

It broke my heart and made me all the more thankful for him. He did it anyway. He fought to protect us anyway. He didn't think of himself. He obeyed and served, and we are so thankful.

Barak was a fearful man, but God saw his faith and used him. Do you have fears? God can use you!

Samson

If you are not acquainted with Samson, read his story in Judges 13-16. What kind of man was he?

Godly is probably not the first adjective you thought of. Though physically strong, Samson was morally weak. He was set apart as a lifetime Nazirite but never lived by those standards (Num. 6:1-8). His anger often exploded into fleshly rage. He indulged lusts of all sorts. But the God Who had called him to "begin to deliver Israel out of the hand of the Philistines" (Judg. 13:5) sovereignly overruled Samson's weakness and foolishness and used the tragedies they caused as "an occasion to move against the Philistines" (Judg. 14:4).

Samson always knew his remarkable strength was from God. After slaying a thousand Philistines with the jawbone of a donkey, Samson credited God: "You have given this great deliverance by the hand of Your servant" (Judg. 15:18). Samson never hesitated to attempt the impossible in God's power.

But Samson failed often and suffered because he did. Our last sight of Samson is heartbreaking. Betrayed, maimed, blinded, enslaved, he is performing at a Philistine feast like a trained animal. But God's hand was still on Samson. How do you know Samson had not lost his faith? (See Judg. 16:28-30.)

That night, in a dramatic act of self-sacrifice and God-dependence, Samson killed three thousand Philistines. Through God's enabling power, this flawed hero fulfilled his calling.

Samson was a weak man, but God saw his faith and used him. Are you weak? God can use you!

Jephthah

Jephthah's life had a rough start. Banished from his home by his half-brothers because his mother was a harlot, Jephthah became a bandit warrior and the leader of a gang of marauders. "Worthless men [scoundrels] banded together with Jephthah and went out raiding with him" (Judg. 11:3).

Eventually, Jephthah's brothers came crawling back, begging him to drive away the Ammonites who had oppressed Israel for eighteen years. Jephthah used their desperation as a tool to negotiate for headship in the family, then agreed to go to battle for them, declaring his faith in God: "May the Lord, the Judge, render judgment this day between the children of Israel and the people of Ammon" (Judg. 11:27). In exchange for the victory, Jephthah made this vow: "Whatever comes out of the doors of my house to meet me, when I return in peace from the people of Ammon, shall surely be the Lord's, and I will offer it up as a burnt offering" (Judg. 11:31).

God gave Jephthah victory. But his vow was foolish and fatal to his daughter (Judg. 11:30-40). Brokenhearted Jephthah still honored his promise, saying, "I have given my word to the Lord, and I cannot go back on it" (Judg. 11:35).

Jephthah was impulsive and unwise, but God saw his faith and used him. Are you sometimes impulsive and unwise? God can use you!

David

Slaying Goliath with a sling and stone is the story we remember best from David's life, but he had been facing enemies since he was a young shepherd. While preparing to fight the giant Philistine, he remembered his early foes: "The Lord, Who delivered me from the paw of the lion and from the paw of the bear, He will deliver me from the hand of this Philistine" (1 Sam. 17:37).

The stone did not sink into Goliath's forehead because David had a strong arm and accurate aim. God guided the rock because it was flung in faith. What motivated David to battle Goliath? What did David want everyone to know? (See 1 Sam. 17:45-47.)

The shepherd boy grew up to be a warrior who killed Israel's enemies by the tens of thousands. He always gave God credit for his victories, for he knew they came only through God's power. What did David do before going into battle? (See 1 Sam. 23:2, 10-12; 2 Sam. 5:19.)

King Saul's hostility gave David another opportunity to show his faith. What kept David calm when this bitter man was trying to kill him? (See 1 Sam. 24:12, 15.)

David was not perfect. We are appalled when we read about his sin with Bathsheba, his betrayal of her husband's trust, and the lying and arranged murder that followed. God was grieved by David's sin, but He did not forsake him, especially in light of David's repentance. David turned his regret and restoration into a song.

> I acknowledge my transgressions, and my sin is always before me. Against You, You only, have I sinned, and done this evil in Your sight. . . . Purge me with hyssop, and I shall be clean; wash me, and I shall be whiter than snow. . . . Hide Your face from my sins, and blot out all my iniquities. (Psa. 51:3, 4, 7, 9)

Faith in God's mercy gave David confidence that he would be forgiven and made useful again.

> The sacrifices of God are a broken spirit, a broken and a contrite heart—these, O God, You will not despise. (Psa. 51:17)

> Restore to me the joy of Your salvation, and uphold me by Your generous Spirit. Then I will teach transgressors Your ways, and sinners shall be converted to You. Deliver me from the guilt of bloodshed, O God, the God of my salvation, and my tongue shall sing aloud of Your righteousness. (Psa. 51:12-14)

When you are smothered by guilt and convinced of your worthlessness, faith in God's character will lift your heart.

David was a sinful man, but God saw his faith and used him. Are you sinful? God can use you!

Samuel

God gave baby Samuel to Hannah, and she gave him back to God. Samuel's first encounter with God came when he was a little boy living with the priest Eli. Read 1 Samuel 3:1-18. What a moment it was when he heard God call his name. What faith it took for a small child to believe that the voice in the night came from Jehovah. And what a perfect response Samuel gave: "Speak, for Your servant hears." (1 Sam. 3:10). All his life, Samuel did what God asked.

Samuel had the scary job of telling Eli that because of his sons' vile sins, Eli's family was doomed. Though Samuel was "afraid to tell Eli the vision" (1 Sam. 3:15), he "told him everything, and hid nothing from him" (1 Sam. 3:18). God trusted Samuel to faithfully speak the truth.

From the days of King Saul's anointing and coronation to his disobedience and dethroning, Samuel was the one sent to confront Saul. Saul was unstable, so it was a risky job. But faithful Samuel did what the Lord said (1 Sam. 16:4). Over the years Samuel delivered hard messages to people who did not want to hear them. Soon "all Israel from Dan to Beersheba knew that Samuel had been established as a prophet of the Lord" (1 Sam. 3:20).

Samuel obeyed the voice of God. God saw his faith and used him. Do you obey God? He can use you!

The prophets

A Bible prophet was someone who heard a revelation from God—a warning, a special message, or a forecast of the future—and by speaking or writing, passed it along to others. You have heard of the prophets Elijah and Elisha, Isaiah and Jeremiah and Daniel, but there were many more, unknown to us but known and honored by God.

Many more heroes

Hebrews 11:33-35 lists more of the extraordinary victories won by faith.

Ordinary people with faith in God's mighty power . . .

> *Subdued kingdoms* – conquered nations in God's name
> *Worked righteousness* – did what was right even when it was hard
> *Obtained promises* – saw God's promises fulfilled
> *Stopped the mouths of lions* – like Daniel, Samson, David, and Benaiah
> *Quenched the violence of fire* – like Shadrach, Meshach, and Abednego
>   in the fiery furnace

Escaped the edge of the sword – as David escaped from Saul and Elijah escaped from Jezebel

Out of weakness were made strong – like blind Samson in the Philistine temple

Became valiant in battle – like fainthearted Barak

Turned to flight the armies of the aliens – routed hostile foreign armies

Received their dead raised to life again – like the widow of Zarephath and the Shunamite woman

I suspect that if I knew about your victories, I would add your name to this list of heroes. Of course, our lives are quieter than theirs. We have not had to face giants or lions or swords or armies in the name of the Lord. (Not yet, anyway.) But we each have our own battles and struggles that call for valiant, enduring faith.

A missionary wife gave this testimony about the clash of faith and doubt.

> *After 2 1/2 years of raising support to serve as church planters in Africa, the reality of needing to raise an additional $50,000 more for baggage and passage hit us. We had seen God provide this exact and seemingly impossible amount twelve years before during a life-threatening medical crisis. Now here we were, needing the same amount of money from our Provider, and knowing that yesterday's faith wasn't enough for today's need.*

> *I had days of strong feelings of faith when confidence soared high. Other days, surrounded by the chaos of boxes and piles of items to give away, those feelings fled, and I had dark doubts. My family will tell you that they could tell when I was struggling with believing God, because I would pause in my packing and walk around the house preaching aloud to myself, "God is going to do this! By His mighty hand and His outstretched arm, He is going to do this!"*

Together Deuteronomy 26:8 and Psalm 136:12 became my cry of faith during those months. And in April, just two months before we left for Africa, God provided through one couple the remaining money we needed. Suddenly it was done, and He did it!

Think it through

When God uses fallible people to accomplish great feats of faith, what is He revealing about Himself?

CHAPTER TWELVE
The Sufferings of Faith

Others were tortured, not accepting deliverance, that they might obtain a better resurrection. Women received their dead raised to life again. Still others had trial of mockings and scourgings, yes, and of chains and imprisonment. They were stoned, they were sawn in two, were tempted, were slain with the sword. They wandered about in sheepskins and goatskins, being destitute, afflicted, tormented— of whom the world was not worthy. They wandered in deserts and mountains, in dens and caves of the earth. And all these, having obtained a good testimony through faith, did not receive the promise, God having provided something better for us, that they should not be made perfect apart from us. (Heb. 11:35a-40)

Christians have troubles like everyone else. Being a believer does not mean living a problem-free life. In fact, some of our difficulties arise *because* of our faith. It's heartbreaking and humbling to realize how many Christians have suffered for believing the same things you and I believe. We will meet some of them as we walk through Hebrews 11:35b-40. From this passage we will learn this challenging truth: *faith suffers*.

And others were tortured
This refers to a horrible form of punishment in which victims were stretched over a rotating wheel, or *tympanum*. As the wheel turned, their arms and legs were bludgeoned and broken by tormentors wielding heavy clubs.

not accepting deliverance
Martyrs refuse to renounce what they believe just to spare themselves pain. They love truth more than comfort.

that they might obtain a better resurrection.
Martyrs endure by focusing on heaven. They see death as the door into a

glorious, pain-free eternity. Stephen, the first Christian martyr, was stoned to death. As his torture began, what did he see? (See Acts 7:54-56.)

Not every martyr has the privilege of having faith made sight before death. For most, it is what eyes *cannot* see that gives them courage.

Still others had trial of mockings
The vicious tongue of a tormentor inflicts pain.

and scourgings
Before execution, martyrs have been flogged with leather strips embedded with glass, bone, or metal. Jesus suffered this before His crucifixion. Victims of scourging often lose consciousness or die from intense pain.

yes, and of chains and imprisonment.
Shackles, manacles, stocks, and fetters were familiar to the faith heroes who, like Jeremiah in the muddy pit (Jer. 37-38), rotted in prisons and dungeons.

They were stoned, they were sawn in two
The prophet Zechariah was stoned for daring to speak truth (2 Chron. 24:20-21). Naboth was stoned for his loyalty to God's law (1 Kings 21:1-16). According to tradition, the prophet Isaiah's messages made people angry enough to cut him in half with a wooden saw.

were tempted
Under threats like these, believers face an overwhelming temptation to renounce their faith.

were slain with the sword.
For thousands of years, the sword has been a tool of execution. John the Baptist was beheaded for rebuking Herod's sin (Mark 6:17-29). Martyrdom by beheading is still happening today. On December 26, 2019 (ironically a day set aside to honor the martyr Stephen), a militant group in Nigeria killed eleven men for being Christians. One was shot; ten were beheaded.

They wandered about in sheepskins and goatskins, being destitute, afflicted, tormented—of whom the world was not worthy. They wandered in deserts and mountains, in dens and caves of the earth.

Believers have been banished to live like animals in the wilderness and treated like filthy outcasts because of their faith. To escape danger, others have had to live as beggars and nomads in desolate places. Though they looked like discards from polite society, they were actually living in exile apart from an inferior world.

And all these, having obtained a good testimony through faith

Faith gave them a vision beyond torture, prison, execution, and exile to God's everlasting promises. God Himself gives witness to their faith.

did not receive the promise, God having provided something better for us, that they should not be made perfect apart from us.

Old Testament believers looked forward to the arrival of the Redeemer, but for us His coming is history. They waited for the promised One, while we know He has already come. All believers past and present are one. Someday we will all join to sing praise to our Savior!

Until then, we can endure the same way we have been saved—by faith. Promises like these keep us stable in suffering.

> The righteous cry out, and the Lord hears, and delivers them out of all their troubles. . . . Many are the afflictions of the righteous, but the Lord delivers him out of them all. (Psa. 34:17, 19)

> For You, O God, have tested us; You have refined us as silver is refined. You brought us into the net; You laid affliction on our backs. You have caused men to ride over our heads; we went through fire and through water; but You brought us out to rich fulfillment. (Psa. 66:10-12)

People may mock what they call our archaic beliefs and outdated lifestyle, but few of us have faced a Hebrews 11 level of persecution. If it does come to us someday, we should not be surprised. Jesus was crucified, His earliest followers were martyred, and throughout history the persecution of Christians has been common. This may be the least-popular promise in the Bible: "All who desire to live godly in Christ Jesus will suffer persecution" (2 Tim. 3:12).

This is the testimony of a young wife and mother soon after her husband was martyred on their mission field.

> *I'm completely overwhelmed, and yet I know that the same God who parted the Red Sea for His people is still in control. Right now, faith in His way being perfect is completely a choice. I do not feel it at all. This fire is so hot. Please pray the Lord will give me wisdom and strength for each step, and for Him to overshadow me with healing in his wings.*
>
> *The Lord has put a choice before me, as He does every morning—"Make my joy your strength, and choose to love and trust Me. Choose to surrender and believe that My plan for you is best, or choose to lose hope, give up, and lose out on My blessings and what I have planned for you to do."*
>
> *Each day my precious Savior reminds me that life right now is a choice. I choose whether or not to trust and hold onto Him, when the pain in my heart is greater than I can bear. I choose whether or not to believe that His precious promises are true and can be claimed and acted upon. I choose whether or not to follow in faith and run the race still set before me, looking unto Jesus.*
>
> *The pain doesn't go away, and the tears still fall, but there is a peace and comfort that fills my heart, knowing that "He knows the way that I take; when He has tested me, I shall come forth as gold" (Job 23:10).*

Whether your suffering comes from public persecution or private pain, the truths that will help you endure by faith are the same. Rewrite the following scriptures in your own words. Store them in your heart so they are there when you need them.

Words from Jesus, Who was rejected and crucified.

Matthew 5:10-12

John 15:18-21

Words from the apostle Paul, who suffered well.

Romans 5:3-5

Romans 8:16-18

2 Corinthians 1:3-5

2 Corinthians 4:16-18

Words from Peter, who was martyred.

1 Peter 1:6-7

1 Peter 2:19-23

1 Peter 3:13-17

1 Peter 4:12-14

Think it through

Suffering has caused some people to lose their faith, but others have found that suffering has strengthened their faith like nothing else. How can this be? What makes the difference?

Before We Go

Now that you have learned what faith *is* and what faith *does*, what do you do with what you know? You run!

> Since we are surrounded by so great a cloud of witnesses, let us lay aside every weight, and the sin which so easily ensnares us, and let us run with endurance the race that is set before us, looking unto Jesus, the author and finisher of our faith, who for the joy that was set before Him endured the cross, despising the shame, and has sat down at the right hand of the throne of God. (Heb. 12:1-2)

Imagine the Christian life as a race in an amphitheater, with a track for runners and tiers of seats rising upward like a cloud. Some of the spectators in the stadium are the heroes we have met in Hebrews 11—people with disappointments, heartaches, fears, and weaknesses; people who were faithful in impossible circumstances; people who chose faith over unbelief. Fallible but faithful people.

As you run, these heroes call out to you. *Drop the weights that are slowing you down. Don't fall into the traps of sin. Run to Jesus.*

Jesus is the *author* of your faith—the pacesetter, the example, Who has gone ahead and knows how hard it is.

Jesus is the *finisher* of your faith—the completer, Who offers living water and encouraging words all the way to the end.

The life of faith is a marathon, not a sprint. It can be long, hard, rocky, and steep. It can even be agonizing, as it was for the mother who wrote this two years after her young adult daughter died.

On this mundane day, I am suddenly weeping. I am remembering so much of that cancer battle with all its ugliness. And I am muffling my sobs in a pillow so my children do not hear me. All at once, there are so many reasons to cry.

Some days it's a slow walk through grief, stepping over obstacles you thought were thrown away long ago. Who knew the sorrow could suck you in like that, steal your breath in a moment? That's just the way it is. The path is long, and the suffering slows us. But it doesn't mean we are not moving forward. It doesn't mean there is no light up ahead.

Emotion is not the enemy of faith. No, emotion can be the friend that drives us to our knees. It can open our eyes to present beauty and increase our longing for future rest. It allows us to curl up close near the breast of the Comforter.

Sadness? What is that compared to the faith pulsing in us? Fear? The fast beating in our chest slows as we consider the sovereignty of God. Suffering? Pain in this small breath of time will be forgotten in the wide expanse of eternity.

What emotion is overwhelming you today? Let it draw you to the One who suffered for you and is touched with every aspect of your suffering. Let your longing lead you to the One who delivers and saves. Let it lead you to the cross and to the Savior. Let your soul be stilled.

No matter what the crisis, you can choose faith over doubt. You can run toward Jesus one step at a time. When you finally see Him face to face (1 Cor. 13:12), there will be no more need for faith, for all will be made sight. But until that day, see the invisible and live by faith in what you see.

Acknowledgements

I am grateful to the friends and family members who have generously allowed me to share their faith challenges with you in their own words, originally shared through social media posts or in personal correspondence. These anonymous heroes of faith are honored by God and by me.

And for her invaluable editing skills, my heartfelt thanks go to Rachelle Miller.

Made in the USA
Columbia, SC
22 December 2022

73569927R00065